DAZZLE ME!

HOW TO DELIVER UNCOMMONLY GOOD CUSTOMER SERVICE EVERY TIME

BY THE EDITORS AT DARTNELL

WRITER: DAVID DEE

ILLUSTRATOR: MICHAEL KLEIN

Dartnell is a publisher serving the world of business with books, manuals, newsletters, and training materials for executives, managers, supervisors, salespeople, financial officials, personnel executives, and office employees. Dartnell also produces management and sales training videos and audiocassettes, and publishes many useful business forms, and many of its materials and films are available in languages other than English. Dartnell, established in 1917, serves the world's business community. For details, catalogs, and product information, write to:

THE DARTNELL CORPORATION
4660 N Ravenswood Ave
Chicago, IL 60640-4595, U.S.A.
Or phone (800) 621-5463 in U.S. and Canada
www.dartnellcorp.com

This publication is designed to provide accurate and authoritative information in regard to the subject matter covered. It is sold with the understanding that the publisher is not engaged in rendering legal, accounting, or other professional service. If legal advice or other expert assistance is required, the services of a competent professional person should be sought.

*—From a Declaration of Principles jointly
adopted by a Committee of the American Bar Association
and a Committee of Publishers.*

© Copyright 1997
in the United States, Canada, and Britain by
THE DARTNELL CORPORATION

ISBN 0-85013-274-6

Library of Congress Catalog Card Number 97-065283

Printed in the United States of America by The Dartnell Press,
Chicago, IL 60640-4595

CONTENTS

PART 2

CHAPTER 4

CHAPTER 5

THE DAZZLE ME! FORMULA
STEP 2: BE FRIENDLY

CHAPTER 6

CHAPTER 7

THE *DAZZLE ME!* FORMULA

CHAPTER 8

CHAPTER 9

CHAPTER 10

INTRODUCTION

Imagine a lightbulb going off above the headquarters of business organizations across the United States. That's what it was like in the mid-1980s, when company presidents, CEOs, managers, and supervisors suddenly woke up to the importance of customer service.

This revelation came on the heels of the quality improvement movement that hit many companies in the early 1980s. Initially, many businesses thought of quality only in terms of the products they produced. Organization after organization put systems into place that resulted in better widgets that were produced faster and more efficiently.

But the more successful organizations realized that quality improvement requires an *organizationwide* commitment. In all the concern for quality improvement, many companies had overlooked the most important ingredient — the customer. That's when those lightbulbs started going off. Enlightened business leaders who had assumed that "if you build a better widget, they will come" suddenly realized that they had to do even *more*: They had to stand behind their products with high-quality customer service as well.

About this time, lightbulbs were going off elsewhere. Customers began to realize that they now had a wide range of options as to where they could shop, what products to buy, and what services they would pay for. If they didn't get satisfaction in one place, they could go somewhere else. And, today, that demand for the absolute *best* service is the watchword of nearly all customers. If the level of service they expect isn't met by one company, another will welcome them with open arms and *dazzle* them with good service.

As a result, customer service, like other professions, has become much more sophisticated and demanding. Reps who provide only average service won't go very far, while the sky is now the limit for those who make a personal commitment to *dazzle* customers with *uncommonly* good customer service every time.

If you are one of those reps — someone who wants to grow personally and professionally, who wants your company to stand out from the rest, who wants to go beyond just "pleasing" customers to dazzling them instead — this book can help get you there.

HOW TO USE *DAZZLE ME!*

This book is divided into two parts. In Part 1, *Dazzle Me!* leads you through an overview of basic customer service concepts and techniques. For new service reps, this is an opportunity to understand the importance of making a commitment to top-notch customer service, the value of understanding customers and their needs, and the importance of "selling" your customers on service. For the more experienced rep, this section is a quick refresher and a source for tips and motivation.

In Part 2, you'll learn the *Dazzle Me!* 7-Step Formula for Frontline Success, for delivering uncommonly good service every time. You'll learn how to:

1. **Be fast.** Respond quickly in person and on the telephone.

2. **Be friendly.** Attitude is everything.

3. **Be flexible.** Saying "No" is easy; what can you do for customers?

4. **Be focused and unflappable.** Don't let angry customers get the best of you.

5. **Be a fixer.** The key to handling customer problems successfully.

6. **Follow up...Follow up...Follow up.** Nothing is more important than delivering on your promises.

7. **Have fun! (and put your stress to rest).** Keep cool, calm, and collected, and enjoy the work you do.

Don't be misled by the "catchy" simplicity of the *Dazzle Me!* formula! Each chapter is packed with:

- Dozens of techniques;
- Profiles of top-notch service providers ("*Dazzlers*");
- "What would you do?" self-checks;
- Self-quizzes;
- Quick Tips, humorous — but relevant — illustrations;
- New ideas ("*Service Sparklers*") that have worked for other reps.

With its convenient size, we hope you will treat this book as a "hands-on" tool for helping you advance further in your customer service career — either "up the ladder" or in improving your service every day. Keep it close at hand, and pick it up frequently to uncover some new idea that will help you provide the service that won't just please customers, but leave them *dazzled*!

Part 1

The Importance of Delivering Uncommonly Good Customer Service Every Time

Chapter 1

MAKE A PERSONAL COMMITMENT TO DELIVER UNCOMMONLY GOOD CUSTOMER SERVICE

A company that believes "customer satisfaction" is its primary goal is on its way out of business. It's not enough in today's quality culture to meet the customers' expectations; to be an industry leader, it is imperative that you exceed their expectations and leave them with a <u>wow</u>!

— RICHARD LOUGHLIN, PRESIDENT AND CEO, CENTURY 21 REAL ESTATE CORP.

INTRODUCTION

There it was, splashed across the television screen in big bold letters: **WHY IS SERVICE SO BAD?**

The accompanying news story examined many facets of service in the United States and included personal interviews with a number of customers, asking them to rate the quality of service in general. The verdict was not good for customer service reps. Almost unanimously, customers said "service is not what it used to be" and shared personal horror stories of poor treatment by service reps. No one, from the corner newsboy to the president of an airline, was spared criticism for not treating customers as well as they ought to be treated.

What can be done to change the public perception about customer service? Many of the solutions involve policies or procedures that are beyond the control of the average employee. But one solution you can put into action is this: Make a personal commitment to offer customers the kind of service they believe no longer exists!

In this chapter, we'll show you _how_.

WHAT WOULD YOU DO?

You've been told by your supervisor to "go the extra mile" for customers. That <u>sounds</u> good — but you have no idea exactly what that means!

THE *DAZZLE ME!* SOLUTION
DELIVER SURPRISINGLY SUPERIOR SERVICE

"Go the extra mile for customers" is another way of saying, "Surprise customers by doing something extra for them." If you make a personal commitment to surprise your customers, you'll have gone a long way to providing service that far exceeds the service *average* reps provide.

Here are four ways you can achieve this simple personal goal:

- **Surprise customers by always being courteous.** Treat customers the way you like to be treated when you're the customer. Kevin Orchard, who handles billing claims for an HMO, says, "At the end of the day, if I'm not careful, I'm not as courteous and patient with callers as I'd like to be." So he pretends that each call is actually the first call of the day. "It's a little game I play to help me give *each* customer all the energy and enthusiasm I gave the first call that morning," he says.

- **Surprise customers by doing more than they ask for.** When Karla Gleason returned a spoiled item to the grocery store, the manager not only apologized and gave her a replacement, but he also refunded the $15 she had spent that day on her groceries.

  Karla used that experience at her job at an airline reservation desk. "Obviously I can't be giving away flights," she says. "But I try to make each customer interaction special, something the customer will remember." For example, during the holidays, she stayed 40 minutes past her shift to find a seat for a homebound college student whose seat had been bumped by another airline.

- **Surprise customers by taking pride in your work.** While Valerie Alverez was in line at a fast-food restaurant, a customer grumbled about the slow service and said, "I guess that's all you can expect when people are getting paid only four bucks an hour." Valerie went back to her own customer service job with a renewed service of commitment. "It's true that some of us in service may be underpaid," she says. "But that's no excuse for shortchanging the service we provide customers."

- **Surprise customers who have come to expect the worst by always being professional in your dress and manner.** Speak of your work with a sense of pride. Show a positive, pleasant attitude. Give customers a friendly smile, call them by name, and do everything possible to make their experience with your company a pleasant one.

SELF-STARTERS HAVE THE CUSTOMER SERVICE EDGE

If you're a self-starter, you have a decided advantage as a service professional. You're flexible in dealing with a wide variety of people, you take responsibility for solving service-related problems, and you're not afraid to take the initiative when you're empowered to do so.

Maintaining the strong internal motivation that drives self-starters can be a daily challenge if you're in a high-tempo service job. These reminders may help you stay motivated:

- **Make sure you fully understand what's expected of you.** You'll feel more motivated to live up to expectations when you know exactly what they are. For example, which types of service problems are you expected to handle on your own? What decisions can you make without getting input from your supervisor? What are the limits to your authority? When should you bring in your supervisor to help with a difficult customer?

- **Be solution-oriented.** This will help you maintain an "I can do it" mind-set. Always be ready to propose solutions when you point out a problem, either to your boss or your team.

- **Take the initiative in problem prevention.** Suggest changes you think can prevent the errors or problems that damage customer loyalty. Sometimes experience will have taught you that a certain problem is likely to recur. Speak up and/or take action before the situation reaches crisis proportions.

- **Be alert to problems that urgently need solving.** Don't leave it to others to take action by thinking, "Someone else will report it." The self-starter will notice, for instance, the first complaint about an icy parking lot. He or she will then report the problem immediately, before a customer comes in and says, "I just slipped and fell on a patch of ice in your parking lot."

- **Speak up when you perceive a need for significant change or improvement in systems or procedures.** If you notice customers repeatedly having problems filling out a form, for example, do more than just sympathize — offer help. Keep track of how often it happens during a specific time period. Then, notify the appropriate person: "In the past week, 13 customers have said they find parts of this form confusing. Specifically ..."

- **Embrace challenge.** When faced with a tough task — or one you've never tackled before — approach it as a challenge. Think of ways you can use your strengths — skills, abilities, experience — to meet that challenge. This will motivate you far more than if you approach the situation second-guessing yourself: "This could be difficult. ... I'm not sure I can handle it." Instead, always welcome the opportunity to push yourself past your comfort zone to new levels of knowledge and competence.

- **Commit yourself to continuous education.** Take advantage of any formal training or other learning experiences available through your company. Customers and co-workers as well as people at all levels of your organization can teach you a great deal, if you're receptive.

Meet a Customer Service Dazzler

THELMA LANE: DAZZLING CUSTOMERS AT SEARS FOR 32 YEARS

"**W**atch Thelma." That's what office manager Kathy Karriker tells new employees at the Sears store in Springfield, Missouri.

Thelma is Thelma Lane, a 32-year veteran of the store who is something of a living legend to customers and co-workers alike.

Explains Kathy: "There's no one like Thelma. She makes every customer feel special. She is a 'people person' who wins over even the most difficult customer. And though she is 74 and I am 41, she can run circles around me."

For her many years of extraordinary service, Lane earned an Honorable Mention in the Dartnell Customer Service Heroes Program.

Lane began work at Sears in the early 1960s, retiring, despite the protest of customers and co-workers, when she was 65. But after a year and a half, "I realized Sears was my home. I missed the people," Thelma says. When she asked if she could come back, she was welcomed with open arms.

She's been back pleasing customers for seven years. Now stationed at the customer service desk, Thelma juggles duties: She handles the switchboard (with seven incoming and four internal lines), completes sales reports, and deals with returns, customer questions, and complaints.

Once, Karriker recalls, a woman called the store demanding a refund for furniture she had ordered. "For some reason, this customer was enraged, calling Thelma every name in the book. Even when Thelma promised the woman that her refund check would be mailed the day the furniture was returned to the store, the woman didn't believe her and was calling her a liar and everything else."

Through it all, Thelma kept her cool. She saw that the check was written on the day promised and then personally mailed the check at the post office. "That customer called and apologized to Thelma," says Kathy. "That's not at all uncommon. That's how good Thelma is."

"I listen to the customer and I try to help," Thelma explains. "I try stay calm. If an upset customer sees that you're remaining calm, it might make them stop and think, and then they'll calm down too."

LET YOUR SERVICE DEFINE QUALITY

Quality. "It's a nice word and all, but what does it mean?" a frustrated customer service rep asked recently as she sipped coffee from her "Quality" coffee mug.

Many managers and supervisors talk about the need for quality without explaining what it is and how it can be achieved, says Ken Blanchard, author of *The One-Minute Manager* (William Morrow) and professor of leadership and organizational behavior at the University of Massachusetts at Amherst.

Ask a customer what makes quality in a product or service, and the reply might be, "It's hard for me to describe it, but I know it when I see it." What the customer is saying is that quality is something perceived, or felt, as well as seen.

A recent Gallup Poll asked 1,005 adults to measure quality in the companies they do business with. The top factors they cited were courteous or polite behavior, satisfied needs, promptness, and a satisfying past experience with the company.

Quality, ultimately, is what the customer expects to receive and is satisfied with when that expectation is met. "Quality is more than an attribute; quality is an attitude," says the narrator in the film *The Human Nature of Quality* (Dartnell).

Set your own quality goals. Clichés and motivational posters can help, but you can bring meaning to your company's quality goals through your personal definition of quality. The following are goals for customer service excellence that you may want to adopt for yourself.

Each day, promise yourself:

1. To always maintain a professional manner and appearance.

2. To greet customers warmly and to always make them feel welcome and comfortable doing business with you and your organization.

3. To always be prompt, courteous, and friendly in serving customers.

4. To always adopt a problem-solving attitude when you handle complaints and inquiries.

5. To carefully assess each customer's needs and recommend specific products or services that will provide the highest level of satisfaction.

6. To find the right answers to all customer questions and to keep up-to-date on the products and services your company offers so you can pass the correct information on to your customers.

7. To be familiar with all organizational procedures and policies so you can handle every customer transaction with minimum error and delay.

8. To follow up on inquiries from customers and ensure their satisfaction.

9. To know your company's promotional campaigns and to support these efforts whenever you deal with customers.

10. To turn new customers into returning customers by providing the kind of service they expect and are entitled to.

REPS SHARE THEIR QUALITY GOALS

Quality. Just what does the word mean to customer service reps?

Kimberly Mercer is a quality assurance analyst for Lockheed Martin in Los Angeles. Lockheed Martin reps field telephone inquiries that come into Los Angeles from car owners who have received parking tickets. Besides hearing out caller complaints, the reps answer questions about how to send in fines and appeal tickets.

As part of a training exercise, Mercer asked each rep to write down his or her personal customer service quality goals. Here are some of the responses. You may find ways to develop your own quality customer service goals from their ideas:

- "I strive to always give more information than asked — that cuts down on callbacks. I strive to treat each customer as if I were making a complaint or inquiry. 'Do unto others as you want done unto you' is the standard principle that I find most valuable." — *Maria A. Coward-Allen*

- "Maintain a calm voice and calm way of handling irate customers. Having patient composure has always helped me. Even when they are being their nastiest, I still try to concentrate on the issue in question and not on their screaming and name-calling. I have plenty of customers calling me back and apologizing after they think about how I was still nice to them even though they were rude." — *Ingrid Berrios*

- "I try very hard to maintain a professional manner, to answer calls with a smile in my voice, and to be familiar with all policies and procedures made by my company." — *Veola L. Smith*

- "When irate customers want to argue, scream, and holler, I keep as calm as possible so that when callers think about how they treated me, they know they have had an education on how rude they were when all they got was good customer service." — *Reuben Torres*

- "I believe in being prompt. I rate quality over quantity any day. I strive to be better tomorrow than I was today. 'To be honest' is one goal I strive for." — *Mary Cox*

- "I make sure that if a customer calls in about a situation, I thoroughly review the history of his or her case and pull all files needed to clear up the problem. If this is done, the customer is a lot happier that you took the time to do your job thoroughly." — *Debra Clarke*

- "I always attempt to make sure that the customer is treated as important; it doesn't matter whether the task is simple or very difficult. When you show customers that their problems or concerns are important, and do your best to resolve them, you find that customers are much more friendly and polite back to you." — *Albert Marquez*

- "Quality is to always be professional; to give correct and accurate information, which means to know all the rules and regulations that apply to the type of business; and to always answer questions with a smile in your voice so the customer feels satisfied with your service." — *Sharon Parker*

- "My goal is to help the customer in any way I can, while helping the company benefit from the work I do every day." — *Santos Rodriguez, Jr.*

- "Learning from previous mistakes in every situation that I've experienced — that's how I strive for quality. By keeping focused, maintaining a very positive attitude, and thinking positively, you usually get results." — *Lester Vidaurre*

Service Sparkler

GREAT SERVICE — AND A WEATHER REPORT!

Customer service representative Beverly Stark has a unique way of personalizing the calls she receives at Graphic Controls Corporation in Buffalo, New York. Before leaving for work each morning, Stark watches The Weather Channel, observing the different weather patterns across the United States and paying particular attention to any troublesome weather conditions.

Then, when she is on the telephone with customers, she refers to the weather they're experiencing in their respective areas. Says her supervisor, Chris Keye, "Customers appreciate this personal approach and truly feel that our company cares about the customer."

REPS GET NO SYMPATHY FROM MISS MANNERS!

In a recent column by etiquette columnist "Miss Manners," a reader who has worked in customer service for 15 years said dealing with the public is like "being thrown to the lions."

"The service person, rarely at fault, must deal with [the] snarling customer. Politely. Happily. And produce a satisfactory result," complained the reader. "Service people usually are the lowest paid, the least respected, and have no say in their options in dealing with customers. So please quit bashing [them]."

The etiquette columnist would have none of it. "In [my] experience, the harried service person who casts a regretful smile and says, 'I'm so sorry, I'll be with you as soon as I can' brings out the best in people.

"That service people are overworked, undertrained, and underappreciated, Miss Manners willingly acknowledges. But she wishes you would stop using the argument that you are not responsible for doing a good job because you are ill paid. Those who advance are those who do the best they can under the circumstances and suggest how the circumstances can reasonably be improved."

5 BEHAVIORS THAT KILL CREDIBILITY

We all like to think we do a good job conveying our commitment to quality service to our customers. But the truth is, we might damage our credibility in small ways every day without even realizing it. Don't let your professional integrity suffer. Avoid these credibility killers:

- **Keeping callers on hold.** Maybe you can't control how long customers have to wait to reach a phone rep, but once you take the call, it's up to you to keep wait times reasonable. Janis K., a customer service rep, notes, "I know some reps who have this attitude that callers are so grateful for finally reaching a person, they aren't going to mind how long the rep keeps them waiting while he or she searchs for a record or some information." Keep hold time to a minimum.

- **Promising things you can't deliver.** For some of us, not having to see the customer makes it easier to misrepresent the truth about delivery dates, exchange policies, or other matters. "Some customers are very persistent about something that you can't really do for them," notes one rep. "I have to admit, it can be very tempting to just go ahead and promise them what they're asking, just to get them off the phone, even though you know you'll never be able to deliver what you've promised."

- **Covering up mistakes.** Sometimes, you can't avoid mistakes. But when one does occur, don't try covering it up — and don't blame someone or something else. Take responsibility for satisfying the customer. "When I made a mistake at work, I would catch myself responding like I did when I was a kid," admits customer service rep Steve Whitney. "I'd quickly look for an excuse or try to say it wasn't my fault." Whitney now makes a point of catching himself before he reacts in his old ways. "I actually feel more empowered by taking responsibility for mistakes," he says.

- **Not returning calls.** When Sharon Calderon first called the moving company to get an estimate and sign it on as her mover, the sales rep returned her calls promptly. Later, when she began calling about some damage that occurred during the move, the representative suddenly was not available and never returned calls. "Once, I waited on hold while he supposedly was on another call," she says. "After waiting forever, I hung up and called right back. They told me he had left the building." Calderon adds, "My original impression was very positive about the company. But it lost all credibility with me when this sales rep started avoiding my calls."

- **Being disorganized.** If you find yourself frequently saying things like, "I know that note is around here somewhere," it's likely that others may perceive your chaos as a reflection of your abilities — no matter how competent you are in other aspects.

You can't *make* others respect you. You can only earn respect over the long term through your words and actions. Be sure to make each call contribute to your credibility scorecard.

No Need for Heroics?

If you or any of your peers have to go above and beyond the call of duty to serve customers, then your customer service system isn't working up to par.

That's the assumption leaders of the Israeli army work under when they investigate acts of heroism. Whenever an Israeli soldier earns a medal for valor, the heroic efforts signal that something is askew, reports David Lloyd, consultant with Pittsburgh-based Development Dimensions International (DDI). Leaders attempt to find out how they can prevent the need for bravery and personal risk in the future.

The lesson: Meeting customer needs should be a given. If you have to perform heroics to give customers what they need or want, look at the system to see how to improve it.

DAZZLE ME! Q&A: Paul R. Timm
Why Serve? Because It Feels Good

It is only appropriate that Paul R. Timm, Ph.D., begins his book, *50 Powerful Ideas You Can Use to Keep Your Customers* (Career Press), with a chapter titled "Service: The Master Key to Career Success." In his customer service training tapes, Timm emphasizes that there are great rewards — both personal and professional — in providing outstanding service to customers.

"Providing great customer service is a triple win," says Timm, a professor at the Marriott School of Management at Brigham Young University. "Your customers feel good, your organization prospers, and you feel good." We interviewed Timm recently to learn more about what he claims are the rewards of good customer service.

Q: **Readers sometimes ask Dartnell editors, "Why should we listen to the experts you quote in your publications? Have they ever served customers on the phone?" What can we tell them?**

A: *I was a manager for Bell South Telephone in Orlando for four years. This was when Disney World was being built. There was a tremendous influx of people to the area, and everyone was frustrated because the phone company couldn't provide service fast enough. So, I've had some experience with frustrated, impatient customers.*

Q: **In *50 Powerful Ideas*, you say, "The best reason to give good service is that it makes you feel better." What do you mean?**

A: *If customers expect that they're going to be treated poorly, they become defensive and begin treating you, the employee, poorly. Very few people can put up with the day-to-day barrage of unhappy customers who expect to be treated poorly.*

Q: **What's the alternative?**

A: *Choose to provide* outstanding *customer service instead. No one can force another person to give good service beyond the most rudimentary mechanical levels. But when we choose to give of ourselves — to apply the power of customer service — we feel a tremendous sense of satisfaction. Then, a job can be fun and rewarding.*

Q: **A cynic might say that most customer service jobs don't pay enough for all that extra effort.**

A: *But there are other rewards, like the satisfaction you feel for acting professionally on the job. And providing good customer service is really teaching you how to get along with people. Those skills are widely applicable to all the relationships in our lives, personal and professional. Customer service professionalism is a skill that is always in great demand.*

Q: **You've said that providing good service can be "fun." How's that?**

A: *For most people, true fun is equated with satisfaction. It's fun to feel good about something you've accomplished. It's fun to know you have the power to give of yourself to achieve team success. It's fun to grow as a person and develop new skills and abilities and to know you're increasing in value every day through your experience and learning.*

The choice of whether or not your customer service job will be fun and fulfilling rests squarely on you. If your job isn't mostly fun to you now, it may be because your perspective is holding you back.

HONOR CUSTOMER 'RIGHTS'

Customers are your most important asset. And, as such, they have certain "rights," and it's your job to uphold those rights. No commitment to quality service will succeed if any of these rights are trampled on, says Richard A. Feinberg, head of Purdue University's department of consumer sciences and retailing. So, here are the customers' top "rights" and your top service concerns.

Customers have the right to:

- **Receive a "wow."** Because so many aspects of life are stressful, Feinberg contends, shopping for just about anything should be fun. "You should provide service so incredible that patrons will exclaim, 'Wow!'"

- **Hear "yes."** Says Feinberg, "When customers are told 'We can't do that,' they'll walk out and spend their money elsewhere. You must solve problems immediately."

- **Complain and get satisfaction.** Consumers may be mad as hell, but many are still taking it. Soon, Feinberg warns, they won't tolerate it any longer and will seek revenge through patronage to your competitors.

- **Expect that everyone will work to serve them.** Anyone who interacts with a customer represents the entire company. If you need help to meet your patrons' requests, ask for it.

- **Have the job done properly the first time — and every time.** "The biggest complaint about repair and delivery service is that it wasn't done right the first time," Feinberg says. "Nothing irks a customer more than to buy a defective product and waste time returning it."

- **Be treated with respect.** For example, interrupting a sales transaction to answer the phone is rude and irresponsible. Work out a list of "service rules" to prevent such disrespect.

- **Receive fast service, not to wait in line.** Waiting wins the "bad-practice trophy" and rates as the #1 consumer complaint, Feinberg reports. "Everyone's time is precious," he asserts. "No one should be forced to wait more than a few minutes."

10 CHARACTERISTICS OF TOP PERFORMERS

What does it take to excel in customer service? The H.R. Chally Group, a research firm, has established 10 characteristics — based on its studies — that predict who will be top performers in customer service.

The Chally Group describes top-notch customer service reps as follows:

1. **They are optimistic and enthusiastic.** Reps with these characteristics expect positive results and will "hang in there" during tough times. They find that their optimism is a self-fulfilling prophecy and that it usually spreads to other reps — and to their customers.

2. **They have a positive mental attitude.** When you have a positive attitude, you look at the bright side of a situation and tend to be solution-oriented. Negative events have little impact on you.

3. **They are competitive.** Surprised? Actually, a competitive spirit helps reps succeed. They compete with themselves to improve on the job. Though they enjoy competing with others ("I'll take more calls than anyone else today!"), they know how to accept defeat. They see competition as a means for motivating themselves to do better.

4. **They are people-oriented.** Customer service involves two persons — you and a customer. You have to enjoy interaction to succeed in customer service. The most successful reps are genuinely interested in people.

5. **They have inquiring minds.** Reps with inquiring minds enjoy problem solving. They can recognize and define problems and select pertinent information for solutions. Their curiosity will often lead to a new sale because they help customers uncover needs they otherwise might not have been aware of.

6. **They are organized.** Well-organized people strive for accurate information because they need to perform tasks correctly to feel comfortable with themselves. When these reps make a promise, the customer can feel assured the rep will deliver.

7. **They enjoy their customers.** Reps who enjoy customers put their own egos and concerns aside to see that a customer is happy.

8. **They have developed decision-making accuracy.** These reps know how to gather all the information they need before making a decision. They know how to make decisions that are compatible with their company's overall goals.

9. **They are communicators.** They have developed their skills to make points in a clear, logical, and interesting manner. These reps know how to focus on what a customer is saying and ask questions. This kind of rep can respond quickly to a customer's questions and needs.

10. **They know their product!** Successful service reps have strong people skills, but they also have a thorough knowledge of their company's products or services. They know how to show customers how their needs can be met by what their business offers. Their enthusiasm coupled with their knowledge is a winning combination.

YOU'RE IN THE WRONG BUSINESS IF . . .

You need constant spoken signs of appreciation from the customers you are helping.

Customers justifiably *expect* their problems to be resolved. We can't expect them to appreciate what we do.

You like a peaceful work environment.

Consider becoming a librarian. Few customer service jobs offer peace and quiet. One former customer service rep observed that his work pace slowed down and the noise level became lower when he quit customer service work and took another job. He became a runner on the floor of the stock exchange!

You don't enjoy helping people.

Servicing people who need help is really what customer service is all about. Enjoying such work will make you successful. Some people are just not cut out for putting others' needs ahead of their own. But that's why CSR stands for "customer service *representative*."

You don't have a special way of handling people.

You can know how to carry out the technical aspects of your work and still not have that extra something special that shows customers you are sensitive to their needs and empathize with them when everything does not go the way it should. How you handle people is at least as important as knowing the technical rules and procedures to follow.

You don't enjoy challenges.

Customer service work is full of challenges: balancing the customer's needs with the interests of your company, doing the detective work necessary to find the source of a customer's problem, taking tough telephone calls one right after another, and displaying a friendly smile and professional courtesy when a customer releases all of his or her frustration.

QUICK TIPS

- **Show you care.** According to *Quality at Work* (Crisp), 68 percent of customers stop doing business with a company because the company was "indifferent to my needs."

- **Be accountable.** No matter how careful you are, mistakes can happen. If they do, maintain your integrity by being accountable. Don't tell a customer, "Well, you didn't understand what I said." Instead, say, "I'm sorry. I guess I didn't make myself very clear."

- **Minimize tracking time.** Keep a list of the work schedules of your customers, including internal ones. List starting and quitting times, lunch hours, and busy periods. Include the best time to catch them at their desks. You'll spend less time trying to track people down and more time actually doing business with them.

- **Make downtime work for you.** When the computers go down and you can't call up customer accounts, use the time to call customers just to say, "Thanks for your past business." (And that's not a bad thing to do even when the computers are working!)

- **Listen.** Listening is an important trait in customer service for many reasons. One of the best is to gain your customer's respect. Careful listening assures customers you don't see yourself as a know-it-all, suggests Dartnell's *Overcoming Objections* sales newsletter. Listen honestly and openly, and you can almost see the customer's respect growing.

- **Follow your common sense.** Dick Garfein, director of research for American Express, developed a set of common sense rules for service. Among them: don't keep customers waiting on hold or in long lines, reduce the number of people customers must speak with to resolve problems, and always make the customer feel valued — not like a nuisance. Finally, "Find the right balance between speedy service and personal attention," says Garfein.

QUIZ

ARE YOU A CUSTOMER CARE EXPERT?

In *How to Really Deliver Superior Customer Service* (Inc. Publishing), author John R. Halbrooks estimates that only 16 percent of all businesses actually deliver on their promises of customer service. *Dazzle Me!* customer service reps do their part by putting into action the qualities that customers most look for in those who provide service. Rate yourself against Halbrooks' "customer care expert" criteria.

Are you someone who:

		YES	NO
1.	Communicates clearly?	___	___
2.	Is understanding and caring?	___	___
3.	Is sensitive to feelings?	___	___
4.	Takes responsibility?	___	___
5.	Organizes priorities?	___	___
6.	Has a flexible mind-set?	___	___
7.	Enthusiastically shares ideas?	___	___
8.	Is a relationship builder?	___	___
9.	Is competent?	___	___
10.	Actively listens?	___	___
11.	Is reliable?	___	___
12.	Has a high level of energy?	___	___
13.	Is empathetic?	___	___
14.	Takes the extra step?	___	___
15.	Is a problem solver?	___	___
16.	Expects to succeed?	___	___
17.	Respects others?	___	___
18.	Turns a crisis into an opportunity?	___	___

HOW DO YOU RATE AS A CUSTOMER CARE EXPERT?

A customer service rep willing to settle for average performance would do well with a score of 12–13 YES answers. That's not satisfactory for reps who strive for *Dazzle Me!* performance level. For them, only a score of 18 YES answers is acceptable. Keep this list handy and monitor your performance against the standards spelled out in each question. Incorporate the characteristics you lack into your everyday service for customers.

YOUR DAZZLE ME! TAKE AWAY

MAKE A PERSONAL COMMITMENT TO DELIVER UNCOMMONLY GOOD CUSTOMER SERVICE

Customers today have far too many choices to settle for anything short of *uncommonly good* service. *Dazzle Me!* customer service exceeds your customers' maximum expectations. And that level of service must be consistent and relentless. That requires a commitment from you. Think about how providing top-notch service benefits the customer *and* you. You'll grow professionally and you'll gain self-esteem and a sense of pride in the job you're doing each day.

WHAT YOU CAN DO *TODAY*

- **Make a service commitment to co-workers.** Make sure your commitment to dazzle customers includes providing uncommonly good service to your co-workers as well. Treat them quickly, efficiently, and with the same friendly manner you serve your outside customers.

- **Develop an action plan.** Set goals for yourself. Pick a date when you feel a particular improvement in your service will have been accomplished. Write out your plan and the different things you are going to do to make it happen on schedule.

- **Sign your work.** In quality improvement, "sign your work" means you take personal responsibility for a job before you pass it along to the next person. Adapt that to your customer service commitment. Let customers know you *personally* stand behind your products and services. Give them your name and phone number and ask that they call you directly if they have any questions or problems.

- **Go shopping.** Yes, you read that right! The next time you're being served in a store or over the phone, make observations about what you like and don't like about the exchange. Did the service provider greet you by name? Did she smile? Did he seem genuinely interested in serving you? Put the experience to use. Keep in mind that if there's something you particularly like or dislike about the service you're receiving, your customers will probably feel the same way when they get that same service from you.

Chapter 2

KNOW THY CUSTOMER

Good service is the store clerk who tells you her store doesn't carry your brand but if you'll wait a minute she'll run to the store down the street and get it for you. Our newspapers report ever-increasing numbers of companies that have gone down the drain. Maybe insufficient capital or some Wall Street raider toppled them. But the probability is that they just forgot service.

— ROBERT WILLIAMS, ASSISTANT VICE PRESIDENT, TRAVELERS HOME EQUITY SERVICE

INTRODUCTION

Who is better at telling you what customers want... than a customer?

In <u>Close to the Customer</u> (Business One Irwin), author James H. Donnelly, Jr. uses his experience "as a customer most of my life" to give insights into how customers think. A professor of business and economics, Donnelly says, "I decided the world could use a business book based on the experiences and advice of a customer, rather than another one based on the advice of a chief executive officer."

What do customers want? Here are some of his suggestions:

● Customers want you not to make them seem "wrong." Donnelly purchased a travel alarm clock that he found impossible to operate. Not only were the directions confusing, but the clock also had a number of features he had no interest in. When he returned the clock, the salesperson was surprised. "I don't understand, sir. This is the <u>best</u> alarm clock we carry." Says Donnelly, "The customer was wrong again. I guess I should have asked for the worst alarm clock." He adds, "Never tell a customer your product is the best until you know what they plan to use it for. For that customer, the best can be the worst."

● Customers want you to take personal responsibility for problems. At a hotel, Donnelly discovered one afternoon that he had not been informed of a phone message that was taken at 8 p.m. the previous evening. When he questioned the front desk manager, she said, "I do not answer the phones, sir." She also said the message light probably had been lit but he hadn't noticed. "Fortunately, the message was not 'You have three hours to claim your $1 million sweepstakes prize,'" jokes Donnelly, "but I wondered why the entire ridiculous encounter had to occur in the first place. A simple acknowledgment or apology would have ended the problem on a happy note."

● Customers don't want to be "murdered." Donnelly went to a store, intending to buy a special pot for a friend. The clerk was on the phone with a customer when Donnelly approached, so he waited. When she hung up, Donnelly relates, "I was about to ask my question when she said (referring to the phone call), 'You won't believe the stupid questions customers ask.'" Donnelly reports that he was stunned for a moment and didn't say anything. "I sure wasn't going to ask one of those stupid questions customers ask." So he told her he didn't need help, "Walking to the car, I wondered how many times a day something like this happens, employees unknowingly 'murdering' customers."

Your job would be a lot easier if every customer wrote a book about what he or she expects in service. But since they don't, you have to use your skills to uncover your customers' needs. You won't be able to dazzle your customers until you know how you can best serve them. In this chapter, you'll discover ways to tap into that valuable resource — your customers.

You want to make each customer feel unique and important, especially if you deal with specific customers regularly. But how can you achieve that kind of personalized treatment when you interact with so many customers every day?

THE *DAZZLE ME!* SOLUTION
KEEP NOTES TO KEEP TRACK OF CUSTOMERS

Here's a quick, easy method to keep track of your customers: Keep brief notes about each customer or client in your computer or on a card in your rotary file. You can use these cards for instant recall when you deal with a specific customer. Consider these suggestions regarding the kinds of customer information you might store:

- **Personality type.** No two customers are alike, so it's helpful to code your customers according to their general personality. For example, you might note whether they are cheerful and agreeable, laid back and slow to react, unpredictable, or aggressive and demanding. As you answer your phone or return a call, check your records to recall the customer's personality. This enables you to tailor your message to deal with the customer most effectively. In the case of a demanding customer, knowing what to expect — and being mentally prepared — can prevent you from being caught off guard and reacting emotionally or defensively. Your job will be easier if you can eliminate the surprise factor.

- **Personal data.** Of course, it's critical to act professionally when dealing with customers. But top customer service pros will tell you that a personal touch can work wonders. If you can glean specific facts about the customer, you can personalize your conversation. Take notes if a customer makes mention of family pets, hobbies, or company activities. This brand of personal attention flatters customers and sends the distinct message that your organization cares about customers as real people — and not merely as a source of revenue.

- **Contact dates.** Note on the card the dates when you spoke with the customer. You can then begin your next conversation by saying, "Gee, I haven't spoken with you since August. How have you been?" or "When we spoke three weeks ago, you were leaving on vacation. Did you have a wonderful time at Disney World?"

- **Customer business history.** In conjunction with the contact dates, you are smart to note what transpired when you spoke with the customer in the past. The more specific you are, the more effective you'll be in making a connection with the customer. Note what problems the customer had in the past so you can take steps to ensure they won't happen again. How were they solved? What action ultimately satisfied the customer? These clues can be invaluable when solving specific customer problems.

Take a few seconds to maintain a customer profile card, and you'll be able to make each and every customer feel special. Why? Because we all are complimented when someone thinks we're memorable. That goes a long way in establishing a business relationship that keeps the customer coming back time and time again.

Meet a Customer Service Dazzler

JIM LAUK: INVENTIVE APPROACH MEETS CUSTOMER NEEDS

Imagine traveling great distances — sometimes across the country — to solve a customer's problem, then discovering once you got there that you don't have the tools you need to diagnose the problem.

That's the frustrating situation Jim Lauk found himself in as a technical support engineer for Huntsville, Alabama–based Adtran Inc. Jim's job is to go on site to solve problems related to one of his company's core businesses — new digital telephone lines. "Some of the problems Jim has encountered on his travels to customer sites have been extremely unique and elusive, and all consequently difficult to resolve without the proper testing equipment," explains Dixie Horner, Jim's supervisor. "Unfortunately, there is no commercially available equipment with the capabilities needed to troubleshoot these types of problems," she explains. The result: long delays — often more than three weeks — in getting the problems resolved. "And that's not what an anxious customer wants to hear," she adds.

Not being able to help valued customers didn't rest well with Jim. "Customers are entitled to have their problems corrected quickly," he says. "It was frustrating for them and for me." Jim could have gone on doing the best he could with the existing equipment. Instead, he got busy. Being a new father, Jim didn't have a lot of spare time. But he went to work anyway, designing and building the equipment to perform the tests he needs. As a result of his efforts, explains Horner, "Jim is now able to write tailor-made software programs that run on his board and will troubleshoot each and every unique situation that comes up."

The new device has lived up to all expectations. Soon Lauk will be sharing the technology with the other engineers in his company's customer service division. His device will enable engineers to study problems and prevent them *before* they trouble customers.

Lauk was named a third place winner in Dartnell's Customer Service Heroes contest for his innovation at meeting customer needs.

Although Lauk downplays the significance of his "invention," Horner believes he shouldn't be so modest. "Jim took it upon himself to design and build the equipment he needs to get customers back on line. Problems with customer systems can now be found much more efficiently and quickly, and that keeps customers coming back."

THINK OF YOURSELF AS A CONSULTANT

A loyal partnership with your customers is the result of acting as a consultant — someone interested in fulfilling customers' every need, addressing every concern.

Information gathering is a critical step in the process, says Elizabeth von Clemm, of Rice, von Clemm Associates, corporate consultants. "The more information you can accumulate, the easier it is to tailor your consultative services to the customer's specific needs," von Clemm points out. "Keep in mind that your goal here is to develop and maintain long-term relationships with the customer rather than just make the sale," she advises.

Asking a lot of questions is the best way to get the information you need, von Clemm says. Your big challenge is to ask the right questions — without antagonizing your customers. To do this, she suggests the following:

- **Seek the customer's permission.** Be honest and direct. For example, say, "Our product has many different uses and, to find out how it might be of use to you, I'd like to ask you about some of the systems you use. OK?"

- **Ask open-ended questions.** Encourage customers to talk by prefacing your questions with, "Tell me about your needs for …" or "Please share the problems you've been having with… ." Use the "probing formula" of asking questions. This is designed to give you three key pieces of information:

1. **Problems the customer is experiencing:** "What's the main problem you're experiencing with ... ?"

2. **The severity of the problem:** "How often is this happening?"

3. **The consequences of not solving the problem:** "How is this situation causing problems for you?"

"These questions help customers identify their own problems or needs," explains von Clemm. "Never tell a customer what the problem is or what he or she needs. Once the customer identifies the problem for him- or herself, then you can start offering solutions."

- **Be flexible.** Every customer wants or needs something different, and you must accept that. "Flexibility also is required when customers' requirements change," von Clemm emphasizes. How you meet a customer's needs now may not be what he or she wants four months from now. It's your willingness to adapt to those changing needs that will, in large part, determine whether or not your relationship with the customer endures.

HOW TO ASK CUSTOMERS THE RIGHT QUESTIONS

Asking questions is one of the best ways to help you determine the needs and requirements of your customers. But you need to be flexible about the questions you ask. One set of questions won't apply to every situation or every person.

It's better to prepare a checklist of areas you want to be sure to ask about. You will determine the exact nature of those questions on a "per-situation" basis. Here are some suggested points for your list:

- **Nature of business.** Is the customer looking for information, a solution to a problem, or help with a purchase? By asking questions, you'll know which role you need to play.

- **Customer attitude.** What has the customer's experience been with your company in the past? Is he or she a satisfied return customer or an expectant first-timer? You'll also want to know if the customer has had negative experiences with you or your products so that you can work to heal old wounds.

- **Time factor.** Is the customer looking for a quick dose of information, or does he or she have the time to go deeper into product explanations or needs analyses? You can often determine this by listening closely to the customer's opening statements. For example, if a customer says, "I just want to know what your average delivery time is," he or she wants just one piece of specific information. Provide it without delay. But, a customer who asks, "Can you tell me something about your new product line? It sounds interesting," most likely wants a fairly detailed summary.

- **Results.** What results does the customer expect from your product or service? If you discover those expectations aren't consistent with what you can realistically offer, be up front about it. Then work to meet those needs in another way or with a different product.

Determining what issues you need to cover with customers will better prepare you for every encounter, whether it's sales or service related.

MAKE CUSTOMERS YOUR PARTNERS

Organizations are entering a new phase in their never-ending drive to attract customers, says Chip R. Bell, senior partner, Performance Research Associates, Inc., in Dallas. Bell, author of *Customers As Partners: Building Relationships That Last* (Berrett-Koehler), identifies the progression this way:

1. *Customer satisfaction*, the first phase, concentrated on satisfying customers' needs.

2. *Customer retention*, the second phase, focused on keeping customers by continually exceeding expectations.

   But with both approaches, customers could still go somewhere else if they find better products or services.

3. *Customers as partners*, the third phase, emphasizes retention and customer loyalty. "You want customers to do more than make another purchase," says Bell. "Your goal should be to have them recommend you, forgive you for mistakes, give you feedback, and help you improve. You want them to take on the role of a partner with realistic and mature expectations."

He recommends the following methods to foster partnerships with customers:

- **Manifest abundance.** Focus on the value of relationships instead of transaction costs. "Transaction costs are not irrelevant, but it doesn't make any sense to argue over a $25 shipping cost with a customer who spends $10,000 a year with you," says Bell.

- **Nourish integrity-based communications.** Customers will more likely bond with your company if your communications are clear, accurate, frank, and direct. Encourage customers to be equally frank. A complaint is a gift that literally cleanses the relationship between the company and the customer. "Beg for candor," says Bell. "When you simply ask, 'Is everything OK?' customers hear this like the greeting, 'How are you doing?' rather than a serious question. "Instead, say 'If you have a few minutes, I really need your help in giving me feedback. We want to be the best service provider you have ever experienced. I know there are some things we are not doing well. Please teach me about some of the things you see,'" says Bell.

- **Build trust.** Being reliable and keeping promises clearly help build trust. But these practices take time. Customers don't start out trusting. Building trust more quickly requires a risk, a leap of faith. "Demonstrating vulnerability may be the fastest way to build trust," says Bell. "Take a risk out of faith that customers will respond in kind — which they generally do. Don't question the integrity of all customers for the one-tenth of 1 percent of customers who will rip you off."

- **Include customers.** Involving customers in ways you don't traditionally involve them is an excellent, proactive way to build partnerships. "This is an uncharted and challenging area," says Bell. "Don't take advantage of customers, but when you honestly need help, ask for it. The customer gets a different level of commitment in responding, and loyalty evolves."

PAY ATTENTION TO CUSTOMERS WHO LEAVE

Haven't heard from one of your regular customers lately? Be concerned. Your company loses a lot of money when regular customers stop doing business with you. In fact, a company that each week loses one customer who spends $50 per week loses more than $65,000 in annual revenue.

"Unfortunately, situations like this are happening every day in organizations," says customer service consultant and trainer Barbara Glanz. "Customers walk in the door, and, because of poor treatment and hostile policies, walk right back out. These same organizations often spend huge amounts of money on advertising and marketing to attract new customers, yet do not realize the significant value of retaining or holding on to old customers."

In *Building Customer Loyalty* (Irwin), Glanz offers several tips for reps to use to help them retain customers:

- **Communicate regularly and creatively.** "Communicate with your customers in ways that will make them sit up and take notice," says Glanz. "Communicate by telephone on a regular basis, following up with them and uncovering problems before they become an issue."

  Many insurance customers, Glanz notes, hear from their agents only when it is time to renew their policies. "If we remember what creates customer loyalty, we realize how important customer service is through regular communication and the personal touch."

  Glanz likes the communication offered by two companies: Carolina Telephone Company in Tarborough, North Carolina, which includes an insert in its customer billing statements with the number of a "suggestion hotline," and Mass Mutual Pension in Springfield, Massachusetts. Through its "Keep in Touch" program, Mass Mutual employees "just call a customer" simply to say hello and inquire about the quality of service they receive.

- **Educate your customers.** "Teaching customers how to use your products and services in the most beneficial way makes them feel proud and valued," says Glanz. Some companies put this idea into action by offering customers videos and published materials about their products and services. "My husband is loyal to the local hardware store because the employees there are always willing to spend as much time as he needs to learn about the task he is trying to master," says Glanz.

- **Interview customers who leave.** "Customers who defect to the competition can tell you exactly what parts of the business your company needs to improve," says Glanz. One reason to find such customers is to try to win them back. "For example," she says, "MBNA America, a credit card company, has a customer-defection 'SWAT' team. When customers cancel their credit cards, the SWAT team calls and tries to get them to stay.

  "Remember, 94–96 percent of unhappy customers don't bother to complain; they simply leave," says Glanz. "The idea is to use defections as an early-warning signal — to learn from those who leave why they left the company and to use that information to improve the business."

EVERYONE IS YOUR CUSTOMER

Everyone with whom you come in contact is your customer, according to Jacques Weisel, a Coram, New York-based customer service consultant and author of *Options from Within* (Kendall-Hunt). "Your supervisor, co-workers, family, friends, and even the people from whom you buy are all customers," says Weisel. "If you don't know how to listen effectively, communicate honestly, show empathy, and respond appropriately to the needs of these customers, you won't be able to successfully serve the people who buy from you either."

Weisel offers these tips on how to deal with your various customers:

- **Empathize with your supervisor.** Don't see her simply as an authority figure who can tell you what to do. Indeed, this attitude prevents you from realizing that she is a human being. This, in turn, makes it impossible for you to see her as a customer, with needs of her own.

- **Communicate openly with co-workers.** Be responsive and responsible to these customers' needs through honest and timely communication. For example, suppose you promised a co-worker that you would complete your part of a project by Thursday but aren't going to be able to accomplish this. Call him, explain the reason for the delay, tell him when your work will be ready, and, if appropriate, state what steps you are taking to make sure this doesn't happen again.

- **Respect your family and friends.** Don't take these customers for granted just because they are your spouse, child, or friend. "You can't be one person at home and another on the job," says Weisel.

- **Empathize with people from whom you buy.** You're their customer, but they're yours too. If you don't treat them with empathy and understanding, you may not get the kind of service you want. Therefore, don't jump down the throat of a clerk who is doing her best to handle the customers in front of you, just because you had to wait in line. Instead, empathize by letting her know that you too have experienced a busy day at work and can understand how she is feeling. "Once you start to do this, you'll get the best service," says Weisel.

- **Treat yourself as your own customer.** "Each of us is our own customer," says Weisel. "Service reps have needs that must be satisfied, just like the people they serve. That's why it's important to be honest with yourself, listen to your deepest voice, and determine how you can best take care of yourself at any particular time." For example, don't dwell on your mistakes: forgive yourself for them. "Separate the act from the person," says Weisel. "It's human to make a mistake. You're not a terrible person for doing it.

"In truth, all people interactions are part of a daily continuing education process that, ideally, can serve to improve and perfect your attitude and service skills."

Service Sparkler

MINING THE GOLD IN CUSTOMER COMMENTS

Isn't a bagel just a bagel? Not according to Larry Smith, founder and president of the Boston-based Finagle-A-Bagel, a wholesale and retail chain. Smith says his customers are demanding when it comes to the bagels his stores sell, and he believes that keeping up with their changing tastes is essential. "You have to know what they are thinking to keep your company growing," he says.

Every day, dozens of Finagle-A-Bagel customers call the company's toll-free number to ask about the product, offer suggestions, register complaints, and provide other service feedback. Those who answer the phone not only listen but provide answers and solve problems. The data they collect are analyzed to follow customer trends.

"The calls cover a wide spectrum," reports marketing manager Heather Robertson. "Customers call to tell us they don't like a fruit-flavored bagel or they were treated rudely at one of our retail outlets. We always take action on their comments."

The customer who doesn't like a flavor gets a coupon for a free half-dozen of his or her favorite bagels. The customer unsatisfied with service will get an apology from the store manager. In fact, Smith might just write an apology note, too.

Finagle's toll-free number is hard to miss — it is listed on all the company's packages and menus. "We think the delivery truck makes it known throughout Boston," Robertson says. "Customers often call us from their car phone because they see the number."

In the early days of the company, Smith and Robertson handled the 15 to 20 calls per week and kept track of what they learned by writing it all down on POST IT notes. "The information we gathered was useful, but we never put it together so we could analyze it," says Robertson. "When we expanded both retail and wholesale, we were afraid that customer calls would just become a lower priority and the valuable information they provided would be lost. That is why we had a database constructed, so we could capture all our customers' comments."

Smith decided to build a database that would enable him and his managers to keep track of their customers' thoughts, suggestions, complaints, and whims. "The beauty of the system is that we can pull up their past comments and discuss them with the customer, along with current opinions. That personalized service is very effective with angry customers who cool down when they see how much personal attention we provide," notes Robertson.

The database is a useful problem solver. Customer calls allow management to track employee performance and identify especially troublesome employees. "With that information, we can provide needed training or even discipline," says Robertson. "We continue to visit all our retail stores and talk with wholesale customers to get additional feedback."

Even individual preferences can be accommodated. For example, one man complained that the salt bagels were not salty enough. "Our data showed that most customers were satisfied with the salt level, but we didn't want to leave one [customer] unsatisfied," Robertson says. Finagle's solution: Ask the customer to give them 24 hours' notice so that a dozen bagels, salted to the customer's taste, could be prepared and waiting at the retail store nearest him.

"People we serve take their bagels very seriously," Robertson points out. "We know that, and we listen to them as a group and as individuals. Our company changes to meet alterations in customer preferences. With the database, we have information coming in constantly and use comments to make needed changes the next day."

CUSTOMER SERVICE BEYOND THE CLICHÉS

Mark Carducci remembers the customer service "training" he received on his first day as a telephone customer service rep. "Someone showed me how the phone system worked, and some kind fellow showed me where the washroom and lunchroom were located," he recalls. "Then, when I sat down to start taking calls, my supervisor said, 'We have only one rule around here and it is this: Treat the customer like a king!' That was it."

Broad statements like those made by Mark's supervisor can be inspiring and motivational on posters and coffee mugs. But without the specific information reps need to do their jobs effectively they amount to little more, warn Sam Deep and Lyle Sussman in *Smart Moves for People in Charge* (Addison-Wesley). The authors advise managers to develop a "statement of expectations" for serving customers and make sure it's seen by every customer service rep. Here are the key points they say such a statement should include.

Even if your company has thorough training, these points can help focus it:

- **Speak clearly, correctly, and slowly.** Avoid industry jargon.

- **Use words and phrases that bond customers to your organization.** Examples: "I'd be happy to take care of that for you!" "Your business is important to us."

- **Say _we_ or _our_ instead of _they_ or _their_ when describing your company to customers.** You represent the company in the customer's eyes.

- **Avoid off-putting phrases** like "No," "You can't do that," "You have to …" "We can't do that," and "That's not my job."

- **Learn your customers' names — the ones _they_ want you to use.** Use names when you greet them and when you thank them for doing business with you. Learn the correct pronunciation and spelling.

- **Treat all customers equally well.** To quote Sussman and Deep, "Dazzle every customer with such thoughtfulness, courteousness, and warmth that you won't be tempted to react to their appearance, age, sex, race, nationality, or accent, or to the size of their account."

- **Treat every customer as though he or she were your first of the day.** "Remain bright, energetic, and positive — no matter what may have just transpired with another customer," advise the authors.

- **Anticipate the needs of your customers.** Don't sit around waiting for them to ask for what they need. "Learn how they use your products or services and be there when they need you," say Sussman and Deep.

- **Be sure customers never have to work to get exceptional service.** "That's your responsibility. Make the call, fill out the form, check the records, correct the mistake, and otherwise go the extra mile to make them happy," the authors counsel.

- **Always keep in mind that customers aren't just buying your services or products.** Sussman and Deep conclude, "They are buying solutions to their problems and gratification for their needs. Your job isn't accomplished until their problems are solved and their needs are met."

GET INTO 'THE SPIRIT' OF SERVICE

To deliver true standout service, reps must go beyond what is required — or even the usual standards of their jobs, says Karl Albrecht, author of *The Only Thing That Matters* (Harper Business Books). Albrecht calls this a "spirit of service," which he defines as "an element of giving — a spirit of generosity that makes people give something of themselves in addition to just doing their job."

Spirit of service "killers," he says, include stress, conflicting priorities, boredom, and simple neglect. Service is killed when "people turn inward, away from their customers as human beings, and start dealing with their jobs only from their own self-centered interests."

Here are some ways to capture the spirit and keep your job fresh:

- **Put the customer back in "customer service."** Remember, the quality of service you provide ultimately reflects on *you*.

- **Develop a service strategy.** Have a distinct formula for delivering quality service, a philosophy to guide you to excellence. It can range from a simple statement like "Keep smiling" to a 10-point personal checklist.

- **Think like a customer.** Evaluate how you sound with each customer, especially those at the end of the day when you are most likely to be tired. Adopt the customer's viewpoint. Ask yourself, "How would I respond to a rep who sounds like I do right now?" If you don't like your answer, charge your next call with a new dose of energy and enthusiasm.

Service Sparkler

NORDSTROM EMPLOYEES: TRAINED FROM BIRTH?

If you've ever shopped at a Nordstrom department store, you may not remember just what you bought, but you most likely remember the service you received. This Seattle-based company is known for its friendly salespeople, exceptional customer service, and unbelievable return policy (every returned item is accepted unquestioned whether you have a sales receipt or not, and whether you've owned it for one week or one year). The only restriction applies to special-occasion dresses. "We used to take them back without tags or receipts, but found that some customers were wearing them once to a party and then returning them," says Cheryl Engstrom, Nordstrom's media relations manager.

But, aside from the policies that make shopping here a treat, the salespeople seem genuinely happy and motivated. "We hire happy, friendly, ambitious people from the start, so we see no need for a formal sales training program," says Engstrom. "Our employees are essentially trained in human relations by their parents and learn through mentoring once they get to us." In addition, Nordstrom keeps employees happy by treating them with respect and giving them the freedom they need to do a good job. Some specifics:

- **Free to roam.** No employee is restricted to showing merchandise only in his or her particular department. "Many times, our customers are surprised when a salesperson who is helping them pick out a blazer runs them downstairs to get a matching blouse and then offers to help them pick out shoes," says Engstrom. "But we give our salespeople the freedom and authority to stay with a customer throughout that person's shopping experience at Nordstrom," she explains. "We also have personal shoppers if customers want wardrobe consultation and advice."

- **Buck stops here.** Every salesperson is given the greatest possible authority so that customers aren't passed around or made to wait. "It is very rare that a salesperson has to get a manager's approval," says Engstrom. "So most customers are assured of prompt service no matter what their needs."

- **Regional control.** Although Nordstrom is a national company, it is decentralized. "The buying, operations, and advertising all happen at the regional level, with support from the Seattle office," she explains. "This gives the ownership for success or failure to the region."

- **A promote from within policy.** "Every employee on the operations side of Nordstrom has worked the sales floor at some time," says Engstrom. "We never hire from outside above the sales level, so our employees know they will be in the pool we choose from for promotion," she explains. "For employees who are willing to relocate, the opportunities are endless."

- **Best of the best.** "We select an 'All-Star' from each store every year. It's tough to become one, so it's a big deal. Recipients of this award get a cash bonus as well as an enhanced discount for one year," Engstrom says. "It also makes a big difference at promotion time, because the All-Stars are looked at first."

"All these things work together to give our salespeople the feeling that they have the authority to control their own income and outcome," she says. "You can't eliminate one part of the program and still get the same results. It's these things together that make up the 'Nordstrom culture.'"

'KILLER' IDEAS THAT CHASE CUSTOMERS AWAY

Sometimes the best way to know how to serve customers is to know what *not* to do. That's why the editors of Dartnell's *Customers First* newsletter recently asked readers to create their own worst-case "quality killers" — what they could do to send customers running to the competition. Here are some of their ideas — but don't try these at work!

- **Quality Killer in the mail-order business.** "Receive an order and cash the check or charge the credit card immediately, then make the buyer wait three to six months for delivery of the item. Program your answering machine with a message promising a prompt return call, or ask the caller to dial a different number and have another answering machine pick up. Screen your incoming calls, choosing to respond only to the ones with new orders, ignoring those that are questioning a delivery or complaining about a service or product. Never send out a notice letting the buyer know there will be a delay in shipping." — *L. Anne Lang, Batavia, Illinois*

- **Quality Killer in professional repairs.** "To kill a good relationship, start before the customer even sends his unit in for repair. Make sure you tell the customer that the approximate time for repair is three days, when actually it is three weeks. When he calls in to check the status of his repair, make sure no one is available to take his call, and don't respond to his phone-mail message. Put a very complex menu choice on the voice mail." — *Sue Hammond, Sony Electronics, Inc, Teaneck, New Jersey*

- **Quality Killer in cable television service.** "After experiencing problems reaching the cable company and a misunderstanding over the cost of service, a customer finally gets cable. Then he calls your office, saying that the service technician disconnected his service by mistake. You tell the customer this would not have happened if he would have been watching the cable pole outside, and you say you will correct the problem as soon as another service technician is in the area, which may be days." — *Leslie Donnell, Donrey Cablevision, Bartlesville, Oklahoma*

- **Quality Killer in the temporary-staffing business.** "A 'top-notch' temporary receptionist arrives a half-hour late, wearing black leather pants and a halter top. She reports to the president of the company instead of human resources. The temp has never worked a switchboard before. It takes the customer half an hour to train the temp to use the telephone system. The agency never calls to make sure the temp has arrived on time and to confirm that everything is going well. The customer gives the temp a proposal to type and finds her making a personal call and filing her nails instead. You never follow up at the end of the day to ensure that the temp did a good job and can return for future assignments." — *Amy Neller, Barrett Business Services, Inc., Lutherville, Maryland*

Service Sparkler

PUT THAT SMILE IN WRITING

One powerful way of getting to know your customers better is by putting your thoughts down in writing. That advice has worked well for Cindy Good, a customer service rep for Conestoga Wood Specialties in East Earl, Pennsylvania. "A handwritten note on a thank-you card can go a long way toward achieving customer satisfaction," she says. "Be sure to include information from your most recent telephone conversation, and always thank the customer for his or her continued business."

What makes this so successful? Explains Good: "The customer will feel as if he or she is more than just another account number. Make an effort to get to know your customers as individuals and watch your business relationships grow strong."

QUICK TIPS

- **Put it to the test.** For some doctors, training includes undergoing many of the tests they will give future patients. This is a way to learn empathy. To understand your customers' concerns, you should personally test the products and services they purchase from your company.

- **Feedback, please.** Routinely ask customers for their feedback on your products and services. Jot down and pass on their complaints and compliments to others who would find the information helpful.

- **Provide small-town type service.** Representatives from Dick's Supermarket, a Wisconsin chain, watch local newspapers and send congratulatory letters to newlyweds, newborns, and new homeowners. The letters include coupons and are followed up with another letter a few weeks later.

- **Personalize your calls.** Pleasantries such as "good morning" and "good afternoon" help convey a friendly impression. But you can take personalization a step further by identifying the customer as soon as possible in the call. For example, "Good morning, Mr. Jones." Then be sure to utilize his or her name frequently throughout the conversation to demonstrate your interest in the customer as a person.

- **Personalize your letter greetings.** The merge feature in most computer programs is so easy to use there's no reason to send generic "Dear Customer" letters these days. If at all possible, personalize letters with customers' names.

- **Don't overlook a firm handshake.** Nothing conveys a more positive first impression than a firm, professional handshake. "It's no wonder politicians develop calluses on their palms," says Stephen C. Broydrick in *How May I Help You?* (Irwin Publishing). "A handshake is the one professional way to use the power of touch."

YOUR DAZZLE ME! TAKE AWAY

KNOW THY CUSTOMER

The more you know about your customers' problems and needs, the more effectively you can function as a consultant and the more effectively you can contribute to your company's selling and service effort. Don't wait for customers to come to you with their needs. Question them. Ask regularly about how things are going. Encourage your customers to open up and confide what is troubling them. More specifically, ask them about problems related to your company's products and services.

WHAT YOU CAN DO *TODAY*

- **Make one new customer connection.** Make the time to call just one customer to ask about his or her needs and how well you and your organization have been meeting them. Next week, call at least two customers. If possible, schedule a portion of your day for calling a few customers and getting to know them a little better.

- **Arrange a site visit.** Even if your contact with business customers is by phone, you may be able to arrange a visit to some of your top clients. Some companies offer tours to the public; others may be happy to show you around. You'll make a stronger connection with your customers when you can meet them and see how they use your products and services.

- **Follow up with one customer who experienced a problem.** Look in your records for a customer who experienced a recent problem. Call the customer to see if the proposed solution worked. Apologize again for the customer's unpleasant experience. Let the customer know you value his or her past business and hope you'll be given an opportunity to win back his or her confidence in the future.

- **Send a customer to the competition.** If your company is unable to supply a product or a service requested by a customer, you can create tremendous goodwill by recommending a company that can. You won't make an immediate sale — but you'll gain in the long run.

Chapter 3

Sell Your Customers on Service

Remember this: People will continue to appreciate and reward warm, helpful service by other living, breathing, human beings — no matter how computerized the society becomes. They will smile when you address them by name or give them information or help they didn't expect. They will tell their friends about fast service by friendly, helpful employees who knew what they were doing and enjoyed it.

— John Tschol, author, *Achieving Excellence Through Customer Service*
(Prentice Hall)

INTRODUCTION

Corporations spend millions of dollars creating — then refining — a product they hope customers will buy. They then spend millions more creating ad campaigns they hope will sell their products. But the greatest tool a customer has is worth millions of dollars — and more. That's _you_, the customer service or telephone sales rep. Each time the phone rings or a customer shows up, you are on the front line — a living, breathing advertisement for the quality of service a customer can expect from your organization.

Most customers have no contact with the executives who run an organization. They never see or speak with those who actually produce the products or fill their order in the shipping department. Their only contact is likely to be you — the person they've met at the counter or reached on the telephone. So every impression they have about your company will be based on their experience with you. The impression they get from you may be the only opportunity your company has for "selling" customers on their services. That's what is meant by the expression, "In the customer's eyes, you are the company."

That's quite a responsibility! But that's the challenge that makes customer service so rewarding. In this chapter, we'll offer some techniques that can help you rise to that challenge.

WHAT WOULD YOU DO?

When you tell a friend about your new job in telemarketing, she is not encouraging. She says that you "just aren't aggressive enough for selling."

THE *DAZZLE ME!* SOLUTION
HOW TO MAKE CUSTOMERS WANT TO BUY YOUR PRODUCTS

Being aggressive isn't the only way to succeed in sales, says Judy DeLapa, president of High-Impact Communications & Training. "One of the secrets to effective selling, whether in person or on the telephone, is to concentrate on making the customer want to buy rather than on selling," she says in *Telemarketing* magazine.

DeLapa suggests that you think back to the last time someone tried to sell you something. "Do you remember how your inner resistance went up? Now think of another time when you wanted to buy. Do you remember how receptive you were — how eager you were to get the information you wanted — how eager you were to say 'yes'? That's the difference."

How do you get customers to want to buy? By understanding their needs and showing them how the product or service you offer meets those needs. That doesn't take an aggressive personality. It simply involves asking the right questions and really listening to what the customer has to say.

EXPECT NEW SERVICE CHALLENGES IN THE 21ST CENTURY

In the years to come, companies will be looking for more and more ways their customer service departments can help increase their profits. For the frontline customer service rep, that means increased responsibility and more opportunities for growth within the industry, predicts John Kressaty, director of customer service at S.C. Johnson Wax in Racine, Wisconsin.

"In the 1980s, most companies were looking to increase their sales base," explains Kressaty, who also served as 1996–97 president of the International Customer Service Association (ICSA). "In the 1990s, their aim is to increase their profit base. And we're realizing that customer service is one of the key assets that will enable us to do so. Companies are now looking to the year 2001 and asking, 'What do we need to do to be leaders in customer service?'"

Kressaty continues. "Standout companies know that one answer is for staff to be committed to delivering service above and beyond the call of duty. Quite simply, the better the service, the more people will buy your product."

How can you, as a customer service rep, help your company carry out this vision of service into the new century? Kressaty has these suggestions:

- **Maintain your focus.** "There's a great deal to distract us in this fast-paced world," he points out. "It has become even more crucial to focus on what's most important to you — your family, leisure time activities, and your job." Balancing these vital elements of your life helps you maintain harmony both personally and professionally.

- **Stay positive.** "These days, you can distinguish yourself in service by your positive attitude," Kressaty emphasizes. It will help you to remain upbeat, he says, if you "recognize that you're empowered out there on the front line — empowered to handle the customer's needs, solve problems, and deal with complaints."

- **Be an idea person.** "Think of how you could be more efficient or do various tasks better. Is there a system or a process that could be improved? How would this benefit the customer?" When pondering an idea, always consider the advantage to the customer, urges Kressaty. "A great idea may be of internal benefit but have a negative impact on customers. The best ideas benefit both the company and the customer."

- **Share your ideas with your supervisor, manager, or team leader.** "Talking upward," Kressaty says, "lets them know you're always thinking and trying to improve things for the company. I find it refreshing when people bring me their ideas, and I get lots of ideas that way."

- **Learn from other service professionals.** Join an industry or professional group. Attend their meetings and conferences as an active participant and bring ideas and information back to your own company.

SERVICE SPARKLER

DAZZLE ME! SERVICE AT THE DRIVE THRU

❝I was waiting 25 minutes in the drive-thru at Taco Bell, and I got fed up. On my cellular phone, I called the 800 number they have posted on their sign. They apologized and paid for my entire order when I got to the window — $7 worth of tacos. Now that's service!"

— from a Taco Bell newsgroup on the Internet

VALUE-ADDED SERVICE MAXIMIZES CUSTOMER SATISFACTION

With all the choice customers have today, the pressure is on you and your company to maximize the service you provide. *Ordinary* service is no longer enough. "Customers have expectations, and your responsibility is to exceed those expectations — giving them everything they're looking for and then some," says Tom Reilly, president of Chesterfield, Missouri-based Sales Motivational Services. "From the customers' perspective, it's the right way to treat them."

Reilly uses the term "value-added customer service" to describe the high-level, maximum service every customer service rep should be striving to provide. Here are some of his ideas for offering the kind of service that keeps customers coming back:

- **Stretch your time horizon.** One way reps sometimes fail to deliver great service is by having a "transaction mentality," says Reilly. This occurs when we become so focused on getting the call completed quickly that we inadvertently view the customer transaction as a "necessary evil" for processing the call. "A better mind-set is to realize that your interaction with the customer is but a moment in a continuum — a grain of sand in an hourglass," explains Reilly. "There will be many more moments, or grains of sand, in the future — depending on how well you treat the customer."

  Stretching your time horizon means understanding and accepting that how you treat customers today determines your future opportunities to serve. "Even small orders today may lead to potential big orders tomorrow," says the consultant. "A small order may be a customer's way of testing you. Happy customers return with their friends."

- **Use leverage.** "This means getting a greater return for the same amount of effort," Reilly explains. One way for customer service reps to put the principle into action is to encourage referrals. "Once again, stretch your time horizon," advises Reilly. "Consider the lifetime value of the customer — how much direct business this person will do with you over the next 10 years and how much business this person will bring along the way. If you become aggressive in getting referral business, you can double or triple that amount," says Reilly. "That's leverage."

- **Be proactive.** "Look at your job and organization for ways in which you can become more proactive in serving the customer. Is it by studying invoices for mistakes? by reviewing back orders to find alternative solutions? by offering alternatives or options for shipping problems? Asking yourself such questions and offering the solution before the customer asks makes your service stand out from the rest."

THE VALUE OF 'WORD OF MOUTH'

"You would have thought I committed some heinous crime or something." That's how Odella Martin describes the reaction she got from friends when she told them she had begun working for the customer service department of a local retail chain.

The problem, Martin learned, was that a friend of a friend had a horrible experience returning defective merchandise to that particular store. The friends all agreed never to do business with the organization again. Martin assured her friends that she wouldn't work at the company if she was expected to carry out any such atrocities. And her friends finally forgave her for taking the job.

But Martin learned the valuable lesson that companies should "never underestimate the value of bad word-of-mouth advertising."

Consultant Jerry R. Wilson agrees. "Every company has a reputation or image. And, every day, people talk about the company, its products, and its services. This talk adds a little or subtracts a little from that reputation," he says.

Unfortunately, customers talk most about bad experiences. "For every three people willing to tell a positive story about your company, there are 33 others who will tell horror stories," he estimates. The problem, says Wilson, is not that dissatisfied customers complain, but that they don't take their complaints to the owner or manager. "They complain to their families, friends, and co-workers."

And customers don't tell others about *average* service. They will, however, tell others about great service, he says. "Ask a satisfied customer about how he likes a supplier and he will say, 'Oh, he's OK.' Ask the same of an enthusiastic customer and his reaction will be something like, 'That place is the greatest. They really give you extra attention and service. Let me tell you what they did for me last week.'"

Wilson's conclusion: "Nobody talks about adequate service. Only if a customer's expectations are not met, or if they are exceeded, will they spread the word of mouth about a business."

The way to generate positive word of mouth about your company is to "blow customers away by exceeding their every expectation," says Wilson. In *Word-of-Mouth Marketing* (John Wiley & Sons), Wilson identifies three qualities customer service reps should cultivate to help generate positive word of mouth about their organization:

- **Friendliness.** "This is not the 'have a nice day' automatic slogans that slip meaninglessly out of the mouth," but genuine friendliness, he says.

- **Helpfulness.** "This involves cultivating a sincere desire to help people make their buying decisions."

- **Gamesmanship.** "View serving others as a game without losers. The object is to win satisfaction. Ask yourself, 'How much do I have to do to win this game? The only way for me to win is to convince you absolutely that I am a genuinely concerned, service-oriented person.'"

Meet A Customer Service Dazzler

ZELARIE K. LEONARD-SALAAM

Compassion and kindness. That's what customers can expect in any encounter with Zelarie K. Leonard-Salaam. But it's her senior citizen customers who have a special place in her heart, acknowledges Leonard-Salaam, a customer service representative in the billing offices of the City of Trenton, N.J., water works. Some of the seniors she encounters are in dire financial straits and have sizable overdue bills. Leonard-Salaam has committed herself to doing everything in her power to arrange payment plans for customers in need.

One particular case stands out in her mind. Leonard-Salaam made special payment arrangements for a woman who came in to inquire about her bill one cold, snowy day. But the caring service rep also sensed the customer's tribulations went far deeper than inability to pay her bill. She talked with the woman and explored her situation further. The senior was living in very distressing circumstances but didn't know how to find better housing. Leonard-Salaam searched for and found a home for the customer. But that's not all. She then spent a weekend helping the woman move.

Leonard-Salaam was recognized with an honorable mention in Dartnell's Customer Service Heroes program for her humanitarian customer service. Leonard-Salaam credits her extraordinary service ethic to her upbringing. She was one of 10 children. "My mother and my grandmother, who are deceased today, instilled in me the importance of giving to others," she says. "It's something I try to remember in everything I do. They showed me that any of us can have personal hardships — and how important it is to be able to stand up and say, 'I overcame this.'"

And yet, Leonard-Salaam's personal faith doesn't allow her to take full credit for what she accomplished in helping her customer overcome hardship. "When she thanked me, I told her, 'You don't owe me. Thank God — he put me in a position to help you.'"

3 SERVICE SPARKLERS

When it comes to delivering great service, the bottom line is that customers appreciate reps who add a personal touch to their service — when they put the "me" in customer service. Here are some examples of people who excel at putting the "me" in customer service:

Charles Gerard is used to getting fan mail as a guest services agent at the Hawthorn Suites Hotel in Dallas. In fact, the company's home office in Massachusetts gets letters about him in virtually every mailbag. Comments include: "He made me feel at home" and "He was so pleasant and friendly." When asked why he gets so many compliments, Gerard replies, "I know what it feels like to be on the other side of the front desk. I just treat people the way I like to be treated." Gerard puts a lot of himself into his job and gets a lot of satisfaction back. That's why he continues to work at Hawthorn Suites even after winning the state lottery. He likes his job, and it shows.

Eddie Webb, a bellman at the Omni Norfolk, was put to the service test the day a guest, "Mr. H.," suffered a heart attack at the hotel's front door. Webb quickly called the paramedics. But it was his service to the guest's family in the weeks that followed that showed his true colors. Webb went out of his way to get the family members everything they needed during their stay and never forgot to ask how Mr. H. was doing. Webb's extra effort meant so much to the family that Mrs. H. wrote these comments in a letter to the president of Omni Hotels: "I know my husband was able to recover more quickly knowing that his family was being well cared for. When I count my blessings, Eddie Webb is at the top of the list."

USAir gate attendant **Tom Grant** took the time to really listen to two weary passengers traveling round-trip from Boston to South Carolina in one day. When the two checked in with Grant for their flight home, their reservations had been dropped from the computer. Their flight out of Boston had been delayed two hours. That delay caused the travelers to miss their connecting flight and resulted in their reservations being dropped. Fortunately, seats were still available. As the two frustrated travelers stood in line to board the plane, Grant called their names and asked them to report to the check-in desk.

"What now?" they asked. "Is there a problem?"

"No," he responded. "I just wanted to upgrade you to first class." By this small act, Grant was able to redeem the airline in these customers' eyes.

Great service people put the "me" in customer service by thinking about how they could make their customers' experiences better — not because a manual told them to, but because of the way it makes their customers feel and the way it makes them feel.

SERVICE REP CONSULTANTS CAN HELP SALES

In many cases, *Dazzle Me!* customer service reps know they must do more than handle information and solve problems. They must act as consultants to customers — understanding their evolving needs and showing how their companies can help meet those needs.

To do this, reps must get to know their regular customers. That means digging for more information, asking questions, and then thinking creatively about how the information they've gathered can help them better serve those customers. For example, suppose you learn that one of your main customers will soon be expanding its offices. That's your clue that there may be countless new ways for your company to increase business with the company.

When can you acquire this valuable type of information about your customers? Here are some critical times when you should be particularly alert about customer needs:

- **When customers call to place orders.** This is an excellent time to get more information about customers' operations and to suggest additional products and services your company offers.

- **When you call to confirm an order.** Use this time to ask whether the customer needs anything else. If a customer is ordering paper for his laser printer, for example, an alert rep might ask, "Will you be in the market soon for a new toner cartridge?"

- **When potential customers call in response to an advertising campaign.** In this situation, you are "meeting" potential customers for the first time. Use this as an opportunity to discuss your company and what it offers and to find out what customers may need.

- **When customers call with a complaint or problem.** Ironic as it may seem, when customers have a problem, it is a good time to learn about their needs and expectations. For example, a company may have outgrown its need for a particular product you've offered in the past. When they call with a problem, you can ask questions that will help uncover the fact that your company offers other products that may better serve their current needs.

Serving as a customer consultant means simply asking one or two questions to get the ball rolling. The answers to such simple questions as "Would you be interested in … ?" or "Can you tell me more about what you do?" can tell you a lot. This added role of consultant does not make you a salesperson. It simply adds further meaning to the word "service" in your title of customer service rep. By uncovering needs and listening to customers explain their changing circumstances, you are demonstrating that you care about your customers and want to continue providing the best service possible.

CUSTOMER LOYALTY MUST BE RE-EARNED EVERY STEP OF THE WAY

Is customer loyalty an automatic payoff for good service? "Not a chance!" declares Lisa Ford, president of the Ford Group, Inc., of Atlanta. "Customer loyalty is developed one transaction at a time," she explains. "In other words, you have to re-earn that loyalty every time you interact with the customer." But simply processing each transaction efficiently won't cut it, Ford emphasizes. "You need to go beyond processing to giving the kind of personal, excellence-driven service that builds loyalty."

She offers these suggestions for building loyalty:

- **Do an attitude check.** Are you doing all you can to stay positive? Don't wait until you find yourself feeling down before revisiting the basics. These include "winning self-talk" phrases such as "I can handle this." Use your break time wisely. It's OK to release some steam over a difficult customer, but don't dwell on the negative customer contacts you've had, advises Ford. Switch them off and think of something positive, such as a recent vacation experience.

- **Be exceptional in problem situations.** "Customers who feel their concerns have been handled well tend to become even more loyal than those who have never experienced a problem with your organization," Ford maintains. Ask yourself these questions:

  - "Do I avoid becoming defensive with angry or frustrated customers?"

  - "Do I let upset customers vent without interruption?"

  - "Do I avoid trying to be logical or analytical too soon after the customer's emotional outburst?"

  - "Before I take action, do I acknowledge the customer's feelings with a comment, such as 'I know how frustrating it can be …?'"

  - "Do I involve the customer in reaching a solution by asking, for example, 'How would you like to handle this?'"

  - "Do I act on my knowledge that customers are more satisfied when they get the solution they want rather than what I want to give them?"

- **Keep up your telephone skills.** The customer loyalty you've built with face-to-face transactions can be nullified if you come across the wrong way on the telephone, Ford cautions. Consider these questions:

  - "When I answer the telephone, do I sound like I've just been interrupted?"

  - "Do I sound like I have something more important to do?"

  - "Do I put customers on hold for more than 45 seconds without checking back to make sure they're comfortable holding?"

  - "When I transfer callers, do I summarize their needs for the next person and let callers know?"

  - "Do I call customers back within five days to make sure they're satisfied with the problem's resolution?"

SELL QUALITY BY MAKING IT TANGIBLE

Your company is justifiably proud of the quality behind its products and services. But, as a customer service rep, how do you "sell" quality to your customers? The intangible nature of quality has caused great difficulties for many professionals, including trainers, marketers, and, yes, customer service reps. But there are ways to show people what quality is so they can reach out and touch it for themselves. Here are some suggestions to bring quality alive:

- **Guarantees.** Understand your company's guarantees and emphasize them with customers. You may have no control over guarantees, but you can help customers understand them and help them get the fullest use of their product guarantees.

- **Testimonials.** There is nothing more convincing than a company's competitor who is successfully using your product. Also, major clients, such as *Fortune* 500 companies and federal and state governments, carry a lot of weight. Make the most of these special customers by asking for testimonials. Make it a point to use them at every opportunity.

- **Knowledge.** Quality reps need to know and understand their own business and their products or service. But equally important is their understanding of the competitor's business. This is where you can differentiate yourself from others in the pack. Find out what the customer wants instead of just talking about yourself and your company.

- **Flexibility.** Being able to roll with the punches is a valuable trait. As prospects throw objections your way, overcome them and answer all questions, responding quickly to objections and complaints.

UNCOVER NEW SERVICE OPPORTUNITIES

Take a look at that telephone in front of you. Of course, you use it to provide routine day-to-day service for your customers. But why not use your phone to offer customers a unique service — the kind that makes your organization stand out from all the rest?

Here's how some companies use their phones to create memorable service:

- At the video store where she rents movies, Melissa voiced her frustration over the fact that there is no pay phone. "It'd be a big help," she told the clerk. "Customers like me could call home and run some titles past the rest of the family for their approval." The store worker explained that there is no pay phone because the store encourages customers to use the *store* phone for just that purpose — for free. "We wouldn't want you to leave without a movie everyone's going to like," he told her.

- The service department of an auto dealer had just corrected a persistent stalling problem in Jackson's car. A few days after Jackson picked up the car, he received a phone call from the service department manager. "How has your car been running? If you have any more trouble, give us a call."

- A florist shop where Ron usually buys his wife flowers called one day. "The shop owner tactfully mentioned that it was this time a year ago that I bought flowers for my wife's birthday. That friendly reminder gave me a very positive feeling about the store and helped me look good to my wife when I gave her an armful of flowers on her birthday."

CUSTOMER SERVICE IN FULL BLOOM FOR FLORIST

If there is one thing Joan Watson has learned as general manager of The Sun Flower Florist, it's that customers are very fussy about the flowers and plants they order. "Customers expect their flowers to be delivered when they want them delivered and they expect those flowers to stay fresh for a long time," she says. But, she adds proudly, few customer-focused businesses manage to live up to customers' expectations as well as the floral industry does. "You can place a phone order for flowers and they can be delivered within an hour. Only an ambulance will respond more quickly."

The Sun Flower Florist must be doing something right. The flourishing $200 million Phoenix, Arizona-based company recently joined with 1-800-FLOWERS, the toll-free national florist company.

Of course, filling orders on time is not the only challenge facing The Sun Flower Florist. Watson said that one of the biggest challenges the company's phone reps face is telling customers what it can and cannot do for them in a way that won't offend them. For example, customers often request a $30 or $40 funeral flower arrangement. Because most people don't place a lot of orders for such arrangements, they aren't aware of the value and cost. "The minimum order we'll accept for funeral arrangements is $50," she says. "You just can't get something presentable for less." But Watson doesn't want customers to feel they're being called "cheap" when they ask for a $30 arrangement. To reduce the chance of upsetting customers, she trains reps to guide them with up-front, but nonoffensive statements like, "Our average order for funeral arrangements is $50."

Customers also need help from the reps when the issue is delivery time. "You can get flowers delivered just about anytime you want — within an hour, the same day, or the next morning," says Watson. For years, she says, florists buried the cost of delivery in the price of the flowers. She doesn't want customers to be surprised when they discover they are paying for delivery, so she trains reps to tell callers, "These are the options we offer for delivery ..." They then spell out the different delivery times offered and the range of delivery charges. Once they're given these options, customers can choose when they want their flowers or plants delivered and how much they want to pay. Making sure your customers know your services is a vital part of meeting their needs and keeping their business. Most customers will recognize and appreciate your efforts.

5 TIPS FROM A TELEPHONE SALES PRO

"There's no reason everyone who picks up the phone cannot be friendly, pleasant, and upbeat," says Linda Richardson, president of a Philadelphia-based consulting firm, The Richardson Company. Her book *Selling by Phone* (McGraw-Hill) offers these five telephone tips:

1. **Always keep energy in your voice.** "Stand up when you are on the telephone if it will help increase your energy level," Richardson suggests. "Stay focused."

2. **Be natural.** Speak in a conversational manner and at a comfortable pace. "No one likes to feel he or she is being presented with a 'canned' script," she says.

3. **Establish rapport.** Use empathetic phrases such as 'I can understand that" and "I know what you mean."

4. **Show good phone manners.** Never smoke, eat, or drink while you are on the telephone.

5. **Personalize your calls.** "Use the client's name more than once," Richardson advises. "And always say 'Thank you for your time.'"

MAKE YOUR VOICE MAIL CUSTOMER-FRIENDLY

Customers can be very vocal if they don't like something. And customers don't like voice mail. Today, anything that can reflect negatively on your company is enough to send your customers elsewhere. "What you don't want is for your customers to develop negative feelings toward your company because they've had a rough ride through your voice mail system," says Margo Chevers, president of Northeast Leadership Enterprise in Plainville, Massachusetts.

"The complaint I most often hear about voice mail is, 'I hate recycled messages,'" Chevers notes. "So be sure to update your message often." When customers hear the same message every time they reach your voice mail, it leaves them wondering: Are you in the office that day? Are you likely to call back by the end of the business day? Will you even get their message?

Chevers adds: "Check messages frequently and return calls the same day. It only takes five minutes to check your messages if you do it often," says Chevers. "Even when I'm on the road, I manage to call in for messages about every two hours and return the calls promptly." That's not too much to expect when you want customers to know that their calls are important to your business.

BE SURE YOU HAVE A REASON TO CALL

Before making your initial call to a potential new customer, you may have little information about the prospect. But once you've made that first contact, you'll have what you need to build a long-term relationship with that client and to give purpose to your follow-up calls.

"Under no circumstances should a follow-up call be made to ask only 'Do you need anything today?'" says consultant Peg Fisher, author of *Successful Telemarketing* (Dartnell). "You should have a reason for the call, a specific purpose, and a good idea of what will be said to the customer."

Here are some examples of reasons to make follow-up calls, along with some suggested comments:

- **To sell add-on products or other items.** "I noticed that you ordered new toner for your printer. For that product line, we recommend that users change the cleaning pad in the printer when they replace the toner. Would you like to include a new pad with your order?" Or, "You know, Mrs. Jones, we are a full-line wholesaler. That means you can also buy all your office supplies from us and take advantage of our low prices. Would you like me to send you our new catalog?"

- **To follow up on mailings.** "I'm calling to be sure you received our supply products catalog." (If not, explain when it was sent and when you will call again to be sure it was received.) If the customer received the catalog, you might say: "When we last talked, you said you were looking for another supplier of laser printer paper. The catalog contains a section on paper, beginning on page 115. Is there anything I can help you with now? I'd be happy to take your order now, so you'll have paper when you need it."

- **To report price changes.** "ABC Paper Co. is announcing a price increase effective next month. Since you've ordered ABC paper from us in the past, I thought you might want to place an order now and save some money in the near future."

- **To report on an order.** "I'm calling to let you know the product you ordered that was on back order is expected in our warehouse on Monday. That means we can ship it to you on Monday's truck, and you'll have the order by midafternoon."

- **To announce new products.** "I want you to know we're going to begin carrying Acme printer toner next month. Since you've asked about that brand in the past, how many cartridges will you be needing?"

- **To indicate product availability.** "You've ordered ABC fine-point pens from us in the past. We've got excess inventory on hand and are offering a special price break. I thought you might be interested in taking advantage of this special deal."

- **To remind about reordering.** "According to my records, you should just about be ready for more toner cartridges for your laser printers. We wouldn't want you to run out of toner in the middle of an important job. Would you like to place an order today?"

QUICK TIPS

- **Deliver when promised.** It's just not good business to ship an order when promised — it's the law. The U.S. Federal Trade Commission's Mail or Telephone Order Rule requires companies to ship orders within the time stated in their ads. If no time is stated, companies are expected to ship orders within 30 days.

- **Isn't that special?** One way to generate more catalog business is to let customers know about current special prices. For example, "Today, the sweater on page 63 of our Fall catalog is reduced 30 percent."

- **Time to call?** You'll have greater success reaching customers if you know the best time to reach the business you're calling, suggests the American Telemarketing Association. For example, call dentists before 8:30 a.m. and retailers between 8 a.m. and 10 a.m.

- **It's an audition!** Forty-one percent of Americans with answering machines "screen" incoming calls, according to a poll by Bruskin/Goldring Research. Try shaping your messages in such a way that recipients can't resist picking up and talking. This will save you from waiting for a callback.

- **Share good news.** Suppose your company has a great record for prompt, on-time delivery. Be sure you share that good news with customers. There's nothing wrong with displaying a little pride about your company's successes. Besides, it's just that kind of information that sells customers on your company's services.

- **Yes ... but.** How do you get past all the excuses and get payment on that overdue account? Try taping a note near your phone, "Yes, but when will we see payment?" Those words can help get the conversation back on track.

QUIZ

ARE YOU CLOSING THE GAPS?

Do you really understand your customers' needs? Many customer service programs fail because companies overlook gaps that exist between them and their customers. Those "gaps" are based on differences in perception between what the customer service rep believed had been presented and what the customer perceived that he or she received. Try this gap detection test. Answer YES or NO to each question.

	YES	NO
1. Have you asked your customers what they need, want, and expect from you?	____	____
2. Is your company committed to providing superior service quality based on customer research?	____	____
3. Do you have a clear idea of how your customers make purchase decisions?	____	____
4. Do you know what criteria your customers use to define quality and determine if they're satisfied?	____	____
5. Have you promised only as much as your delivery capabilities can handle?	____	____
6. Do your customers perceive you can meet their needs and expectations?	____	____
7. Do customers come to you with their concerns?	____	____
8. Do you have a performance measurement system in place to help you identify customer service needs, wants, requirements, and expectations?	____	____
9. Do you have a recovery program to turn a dissatisfied customer around or recapture a lost customer?	____	____

Total number of NO answers _____

DO YOU KNOW YOUR CUSTOMERS' NEEDS?

Each NO answer represents a failure to identify what your customers want. There are many ways to measure these gaps — surveys, examinations of sales records, and focus groups. But as the service rep who personally speaks to customers, you are your company's best source for knowledge about its customers. Use this quiz as a guide to knowing the right questions to ask customers so you can be sure you and your organization are meeting all their needs.

YOUR DAZZLE ME! TAKE AWAY

SELL YOUR CUSTOMERS ON SERVICE

In the shuffle to find new customers, it's easy to forget that a company's most important customer is in front of you or on the phone right now. The fact is, it costs businesses six times more to gain a new customer than to retain a current one. Each time you provide *Dazzle Me!* service to a current customer, you're helping to ensure your company's success in the future.

WHAT YOU CAN DO *TODAY*

- **Make at least one customer feel important.** "The more important you make customers feel, the better they will feel about doing business with you," says Richard E. Gerson, Ph.D., author of *Beyond Customer Service* (Crisp). "Call them by name, ask them to tell you about themselves, and ask questions about their accomplishments. Your reward will be a lifetime."

- **Exceed an expectation.** "A well-known air-freight company claims to deliver your package by 10 a.m. the next morning, but often delivers by 9:00 or 9:30. That's service customers remember," says consultant Paul R. Timm. He suggests a process he calls E-Plus: "It means first, strive to sharpen your understanding of what customers want and expect from you. Then, second, constantly look for ways to give customers more than they expect."

- **Turn on your radar.** "Think of yourself as a sort of frontline radar, an early-warning system," says management consultant Karl Albrecht in *The Service Advantage* (Dow Jones-Irwin). Encourage customers to speak up about what's wrong (and right) about the service they receive. Ask a few well-placed questions such as, "Was there anything we could have done better in serving you today?" Such questions help correct problems and show customers how much you value their opinions.

- **Show thanks.** "Let customers know what you're thinking about them," says Michael LeBoeuf, Ph.D., in *How to Win Customers and Keep Them for Life* (Berkley). "Send customers congratulatory cards for birthdays, promotions, graduations. Keep a list of their professional and personal interests. Most customers hear from businesses only when they're trying to sell to them. Be different. Add a personal touch."

PART 2

THE *DAZZLE ME!* 7-STEP FORMULA
FOR FRONTLINE SUCCESS

Chapter 4

THE *DAZZLE ME!* FORMULA
STEP 1: BE FAST

*A good plan violently executed right now is far better than
a perfect plan executed next week.*

— GEORGE S. PATTON, U.S. GENERAL (1885 – 1945)

INTRODUCTION

It's a classic example of the double-edged sword. Customers want fast service, but they want complete service as well. They get impatient when they think you're spending too much time with another customer, and they get equally unhappy if they think you aren't giving _them_ enough time.

Meanwhile, management expects you to provide thorough service to every customer. But managers don't want calls waiting in the queue, and they rate your performance based on how much time you spend on each call.

In _Dazzle Me!_ customer service, fast is where it's at. But fast means helping customers quickly _and_ thoroughly. It means acknowledging to customers that you recognize that they've had to wait — and letting them know you appreciate their patience. _Dazzle Me!_ fast service means helping a customer, even when you're ready to leave for a break, because the line has grown exceptionally long. It means providing "one stop" service — trying to handle all the customer's questions and problems yourself — so the customer's time isn't wasted being transferred to other departments.

For more ways to provide faster, better service, read on. Just promise us you won't read these ideas too _fast_!

WHAT WOULD YOU DO?

During some of your customer calls, you stay on the line way too long, listening to the customer talk about matters totally unrelated to the nature of the call. You want to be polite and project a friendly image for your company, but these lengthy calls keep you from other customers.

THE *DAZZLE ME!* SOLUTION
HOW TO BE FRIENDLY — AND KEEP THE CALL SHORT

How do you convey friendliness and create a positive image of your organization and still get off the phone relatively quickly? Don't rule out friendly conversation. Instead, allow yourself a predetermined amount of time to listen to nonrelated matters. Only you know how much time you can allocate.

Say you've determined you can allow a minute for friendly small talk. Don't reveal the limit to the caller. But when the conversation veers away from business, keep your eye on the clock. As the time limit approaches, gently steer the caller back to business and conclude the call: "I'm glad we had the chance to talk today. Did you have any other questions before I go?" With a time limit, you'll meet both your goal to be friendly and your need to move the call along.

Another way to avoid "conversational drift" is to establish, early on, the direction you expect the call to take. For example, you might start the conversation by saying something like, "Ms. Smith, I need to ask you two questions about the status of your account. ..." That makes it easier for the customer to focus.

ROUND AND ROUND THEY GO: WHEN CUSTOMERS TALK IN CIRCLES

Sometimes customers talk in circles. This makes it difficult for you to serve them and prevents you from completing your business and moving on to help the next caller. One way to control the conversation is known as the "PRC" technique. This process, described in the book *Powerful Telephone Skills* (Career Press), involves three simple steps: paraphrase, reflect, and close. Here's how it works:

When the caller begins talking in circles, interrupt and say, "I need to make sure I understand you." Then paraphrase the important things the caller has said. This approach ensures that you both understand the key points, and the caller may feel less inclined to repeat his or her comments. After you've summarized the conversation, give the caller a chance to respond or reflect on what you've said, agree or disagree, and add anything you've left out. Finally, close the conversation just as soon as your caller appears satisfied with your summary. Express appreciation for his or her time, or mention how happy you are about the outcome of the call. Remind the customer of any action you agreed on, then end the conversation. Now, how was that for *fast*?

KEEPING PACE WITH CALLERS

Does where you live influence the speed at which you talk?

Yes, say two customer service consultants, and you can do something about it. "Take two extremes," say Karen Leland and Keith Bailey in *Customer Service for Dummies* (IDG Books). "Native New Yorkers generally talk a mile a minute, while Southerners are known for their slow drawl. If you put the two together, the New Yorker is always trying to get the Southerner to speed up and the Southerner is always trying to get the New Yorker to slow down."

As a service provider, "it's your job to pace the customer, not the other way around," say the authors. "If you notice that you are thinking bad thoughts about your customer, wondering why he [or she] is not slowing down or speeding up to your rate of speech, quickly shift gears and move into a pacing mode," they suggest. Then you'll be on the same wavelength!

Service Sparkler

CUSTOMER SATISFACTION IN A SNAP(PLE)

The following incident shows how a company can move quickly in response to a customer's concern and generate a tremendous feeling of goodwill. This story was told by Hyman Golden, chairman of Snapple Beverage Corporation:

A little story about customer satisfaction: When we launched Snapple in Canada, an outraged consumer called from Quebec, complaining that the French on our label was lousy. We called him immediately, apologized for the error, and assured him that all future labels would bear his corrections. He became a customer for life that very moment.

'ACCOUNT NUMBER, PLEASE'

While you want to handle calls quickly, it's easy to develop habits that actually shortchange your customers.

For example, do you answer calls saying, "Account number, please?" because that will quickly bring you to the business the customer is calling you about?

Make it your habit to say "hello" to customers when you greet them. Being identified and referred to primarily as a number is dehumanizing for many people. They want to be recognized for who they are — not what they buy.

Let your customers know that your company recognizes them as people. Treat each customer as an individual.

FAST ON YOUR FEET FOR WRONG NUMBERS!

When a caller asked to speak to Mary Johnson, the customer service rep who took the call didn't recognize the name. After quickly checking the company phone directory, he told the caller, "I'm sorry, there's no one here by that name" and hung up.

The rep had dismissed the call as a wrong number and went about his work. The caller — who had spoken to a Mary Johnson a month or so earlier — was left with a dead receiver in his hand. Mary Johnson, it turns out, does work for that company. Her name had been listed in the directory as Mary Normandy since her marriage to Fred Normandy two weeks earlier. The moral? When a caller makes a request that doesn't make sense to you, don't dismiss it without further probing.

With a little patience and a little detective work, a good phone rep can untangle most mysteries and discover, as in this case, who the caller is trying to reach or put the customer in touch with the right person.

When a caller asks for someone whose name you do not recognize, apologize and admit to the caller that the name is not familiar to you. Next, confirm that the caller is trying to reach someone in your organization: "You've reached Acme Tire Company. Is that the number you're trying to reach?"

If the caller says "Yes," explain that there is no Mary Johnson at this extension and that you need a little more information to direct the call to its proper destination. Ask, "May I ask what this call is regarding?"

The caller's response should help you determine what direction your inquiry should take next. For example, suppose the caller says, "Mary Johnson helped solve a billing problem I had in the past."

In that case, the caller may be asking for Mary Johnson only because he or she had good luck speaking with her in the past. Tell the caller, "I don't see Mary Johnson's name on our employee phone list. Does your current call also concern a billing problem? If so, I'll put you in touch with our billing department. If Mary Johnson isn't available, someone else there will be happy to help you with your problem. Is that OK with you?"

If the caller will speak only with Mary Johnson, ask him or her to hold (or offer to call back) while you track down Mary Johnson. Apologize for the inconvenience.

What about when it's clear that the caller actually has reached the wrong number?

Convey a friendly, helpful impression of your company, even to "wrong numbers." It's simply good manners and good public relations. The caller may not be a customer today, but if you send a positive impression, he or she just may become a customer.

Consider the experience of one caller, who was calling the 800 number of a mattress company but misdialed and reached the 800 number of a national fast-food corporation instead. When the caller realized he had dialed the wrong number, the person who answered the call said, "That's no problem! By the way, how would you like a free hamburger? Leave me your name and number, and I'll send you a coupon!"

Now that's a wrong number that ended up "right" for the caller!

DON'T ALWAYS RUSH TO RUSH ORDERS

Most customers love speedy service. Offering to treat every order as a "rush" may make you popular with them, but it won't win friends in production, shipping, and other departments, as your co-workers do double duty scrambling to fill rush requests and the regular orders. In fact, the added strain that rush requests put on the system may cause overall service to suffer as shipping struggles to keep up with the demand.

Remember, you have a responsibility to your *other* customers — your co-workers — to work within existing company policies regarding rush orders. Here are some guidelines to follow to be sure you aren't overextending rush privileges:

- **Don't "cry wolf" by saying an order is a rush when it isn't.** Your co-workers are more likely to respond to emergencies if they know you ask for their help only when it's necessary.

- **Take other departments' priorities into account when making delivery promises.** Remember that "rush" orders require any number of employees to set aside what they are doing at the moment to fill the special request. Don't promise a rush order until you are certain the added work won't put too much strain on the system.

- **Stay within delivery guidelines.** Even though your co-workers may be willing and able to help you get an order out quickly, you must be aware if there are any outside constraints that limit what you can promise.

- **Don't rush to promise rush service.** When a customer indicates that he or she needs an order in a hurry, don't immediately offer rush handling. First offer the quickest service possible without a rush. For example, normal turnaround may be five days. But from experience you may know you can ask for two-day turnaround without formally labeling the job a rush. In that case, you can suggest to the customer, "We can send this out in two days. Will that meet your needs?" If the customer says that two days is not quick enough, then offer overnight rush. If there are any conditions, including extra charges for the service, be sure to let the customer know.

Here are some additional ways you can show consideration for other departments:

- Give the production manager advance notice of large orders.

- Inform the traffic control supervisor about special shipping requirements.

- Convey accurate information to the quality control manager about customer specifications.

Communication is the key to making sure you don't complicate the lives of co-workers in other departments. They need to be aware of everything that could affect their schedule.

Following these suggestions, you'll provide customers the fastest delivery possible without compromising the overall service you and your co-workers can provide.

As a bonus, you'll strengthen your relationship with co-workers by showing that you respect their time.

Service Sparkler

S-L-O-W D-O-W-N (BEEP!)

Do some customers talk too fast?

Robert Porten thinks so. Porten, a customer service rep with Utica Insurance Group, Utica, New York, has become frustrated over how fast people talk when they encounter an answering machine or voice-mail system.

"When people leave their phone numbers on our voice-mail system, they sometimes say them so fast, it's hard to write them down," he says. Fortunately, his company's system allows the user to replay the message. But his advice: "Remember that some customers don't have the same technology. Practice saying your phone number, and company name, more slowly. This may seem simple, but it's surprising how many people say their phone numbers too quickly."

KEEP IT SHORT!

Wouldn't it be nice if we had all the time in the world for every phone call? Most of us can't afford the luxury of long phone calls, either those we initiate or those we take. And one of the problems is that the person on the other end of the line doesn't always appreciate our need for keeping calls brief. That's why nearly everyone who uses the phone in business can benefit from these tips for keeping calls short.

To save time on the calls you *make*:

1. **Don't socialize.** Return calls that require only giving a short answer or posing a simple question during lunch hour, when the person you're calling is less likely to answer. Leave a message that supplies all necessary information.

2. **Ask complete questions.** Similarly, when you initiate a voice message, ask complete, specific questions, so respondents can give you a complete answer.

3. **Watch your timing.** If you must speak with someone directly, call just

before lunch or right before quitting time. During those times, everyone is interested in keeping the conversation short.

4. **Group your calls.** Make a flurry of calls in the morning, then block out uninterrupted time for work, followed by a second phone session late in the day.

5. **Get to the point fast.** This was the No. 1 tip given in a national survey of telephone professionals, conducted by telephone expert George Walther, author of *Phone Power* (Berkley). The payoff for you: better cooperation, better results.

To save time on the calls you *take*:

1. **Direct callers.** Answer the phone with, "Jones Corporation. Mary speaking. How may I direct your call?" Friendly and professional, this greeting helps the caller get right to the point.

   The receptionist in a doctor's office greets the caller and then asks, "How may I direct your call?" The reason: "If I don't say that, patients start telling me all their symptoms. They're just wasting their time and mine, since I can't help them. If I ask them how I can direct their call, I can put them on the line faster with someone who can help."

2. **Know your company.** Often there is a delay because callers don't know who they want to speak with. The more familiar you can be with every aspect of your company, the faster you can route the call: "We have two employees named Jackson. Do you want Bob in sales or Jim in the mail room?"

3. **Be a step ahead.** By concentrating, you can often spot the direction the call is going before the caller begins speaking on and on. As soon as you have an idea of what the caller needs, politely interrupt. ("It sounds like you should talk with someone in customer service. I'll put your call through.")

   Don't be afraid to be assertive in this way. If you're polite, the caller will be pleased that you have been so alert to his or her needs. Don't jump in too quickly, however. A caller will understandably be angry if you rush him or her off to the wrong extension or department. Instead, ask a question to clarify the caller's needs.

4. **Control nonstop callers.** When a business associate goes on and on, take control of the call. Say, "I really want to give this my full attention, but it's not a good time for me to talk. Let me schedule a time to call back." Or tell the caller, "I only have five minutes to talk right now."

5. **Call back.** When you make the call, you can better control the length and content of the call.

RECOGNIZE THESE CALLERS?

For some reason, certain callers seem to go to great lengths to slow down the phone call. These callers aren't deliberately difficult, but they can make even the most patient rep ask him or herself, "When, oh when, will this day end?" Who hasn't encountered customers like the following:

- **The "hold on while I get my account number" caller.** No matter how much business they've conducted by phone in the past, these customer always forget to bring their account number to the phone when they call with a question or problem.

    "I don't know how many times a day I end up on hold listening to customers shuffle through papers cursing under their breath while they look for their account numbers," says Cheryl, who handles problems with catalog orders.

    Tips: Can you pull up accounts by phone number? Since everyone knows their phone number, this can save time while confirming that your phone records are up-to-date. If you can't access records by phone number, ask for the customer's account number (or the other information you need) immediately at the end of your greeting ("Good afternoon, this is Mary. May I have your account number?") to get down to business as quickly as possible.

- **The "I could talk all day" caller.** "A sense of dread overcomes me when this particular client calls," says Ian, who sells computer software. "He just won't get off the phone." Customer service rep Roberta knows similar customers. "Because we're friendly to all our customers, some customers really want to share their life stories with you. That's OK — but there just isn't time."

    Tips: To bring the call to a quick conclusion, always convey a sincere interest in what the caller is saying, but then add in a matter-of-fact voice that you (regrettably) must take care of other business. Some phrases that might work: "I don't mean to cut you off but our phones are ringing off the hook today"; "I'm sorry, but there's another call I must take"; "I really mustn't take up more of your time. Thanks very much for calling."

WHO DO YOU SERVE FIRST?

At one time or another, most people who deal directly with customers run into a situation in which they're swamped with work and have high-priority needs from two or more customers at the same time. Which one do you serve? Which one do you make wait?

If you know for sure no one else is available to pitch in and help, it may be your decision — not your supervisor's — to make. Sometimes the simplest solution of all is to contact one or more customers, explain the difficulty, and promise to give the matter your full attention as soon as possible.

It's essential to get your personal concern across to customers, to assure them that their concern is a high priority to you and that you haven't pigeon-holed the question or problem. More often than not, your earnestly expressed concern will fuel the customer's patience. If it doesn't, it may be time for your boss to take over. Your first objective is to minimize customer irritation and avoid the conclusion that your service is poor.

Also helpful in deciding how much valuable time a customer's question or problem warrants when you're busy is to look at the situation from the customer's viewpoint. A serious mistake customer service reps sometimes make is to conclude that the question is irrelevant or that the problem is insignificant, and to treat it that way.

The point to remember is that what seems petty or postponable to you may, rightly or wrongly, be very important to the customer. It's what's important to the customer that counts.

MESSAGES TO SEND ON EVERY CALL

In your desire to provide fast service, you may be on the phone for only a few seconds with a particular customer. But during those valuable moments, the caller will be quickly forming an impression of both you and your organization and deciding whether doing business with you is a good idea.

That's why it's important that every moment you spend with a caller is handled professionally, says Tony Alessandra, Ph.D., co-author of *The Idea-a-Day Guide to Super Selling and Customer Service* (Dartnell). Five basic messages should be conveyed during every call, say Alessandra and co-authors Gary Couture and Gregg Baron. Those messages are:

1. I will not waste your time.

2. I care about you and your business.

3. I am competent, dependable, and well organized.

4. I can be trusted to help you get what you need.

5. I am proud of my company and enjoy working here.

"If you answer the phone, you need the time to do it properly," says Alessandra. Here are some of the phone techniques you should implement to ensure that you are sending all the right messages to your callers:

- **Answer calls in no more than four rings.** If the phone traffic is too heavy to allow this, talk to your supervisor about getting some help, advises Alessandra.

- **Be prepared.** Keep paper and a pen nearby, and, "If prices or other information are commonly requested over the phone, this information should be readily available," he says.

- **Identify yourself and your company.** The caller should know immediately who has taken the call. "It not only gives information, but adds a personal, friendly, professional touch," says the author. Be sure to identify your department as well, especially if a call has been passed on to you: "Jane Smith, shipping."

- **Screen calls tactfully.** If a call is better handled by a co-worker, it is in the customer's best interest to transfer it. However, do so politely. Alessandra says it is better to make a request or ask a question than to sound demanding. "What is this about?" is a rude way to ask, "Will she know what this call is in reference to?"

- **Don't make customers repeat their stories.** It's happened to all of us. You call up and tell someone why you're calling. They transfer your call. You tell the next person why you're calling. You get transferred again, and so on. "The right way to handle this situation is for the first person to find the proper person to handle the call and tell that person the customer's story," says Alessandra. "Making customers repeat themselves is making them jump through hoops to get service."

- **Limit hold time to 15 seconds.** "If you have to keep someone on hold longer, arrange to call him or her back," says the author. "Keep closely in touch with people on hold."

When you follow these guidelines, callers will immediately recognize you as a professional who is interested in providing the best service possible, as quickly as possible, on every call.

Meet a Customer Service Dazzler

MARY JO TRAPANI-COLLINS: HELPS CUSTOMERS AND CO-WORKERS AFTER OKLAHOMA CITY BOMB CRISIS

When the Oklahoma City Federal Building was destroyed by a bomb on April 19, 1995, Mary Jo Trapani-Collins, customer relations account representative for CSG Card Services in Madison, Wisconsin, lost some colleagues and good friends. Eighteen of the 32 people working in the Federal Employees Credit Union were killed.

Among the dead was Visa card program manager Victoria Texter; her co-worker, Amy Petty, was seriously injured. The shock of the tragedy galvanized Trapani-Collins into action. "I had serviced the credit union for a year and a half," she notes. "I knew Victoria's and Amy's standards and how they expected things to be done. After the bombing, I wanted to help my friends in Oklahoma City in any way I could."

She and her co-workers at CSG Card Services spent the Saturday after the bombing helping the Oklahoma credit union's Visa cardholders. They provided assistance as well to volunteers running the temporary credit union set up until surviving staff members were able to return to work.

Trapani-Collins and another colleague, Paige Warren in Oklahoma City, also maintained close contact with Amy Petty, who worked from home during her recovery. Petty, now Visa program manager for the Federal Employee Credit Union, has this to say about Trapani-Collins: "She's the ultimate service person. Our credit union has always been very service-oriented, and we expect the same treatment. Even before the bombing, M.J. gave us excellent service — and that's the main reason we're so fond of doing business with CSG Card Services.

"After the bombing, M.J. essentially picked up my position," Petty continues. Trapani-Collins also helped organize relief efforts and offered other assistance to victims of the blast. She was recognized as a Dartnell Customer Service Hero as a result of her fast, conscientious efforts.

"Autograph your work with excellence." Petty says her former colleague Victoria, who died in the Oklahoma City blast, "lived by that motto." And so, she says, does Mary Jo Trapani-Collins.

DON'T EVEN THINK ABOUT IT

Think before you speak. This is one of the cardinal rules of customer service. Sometimes, in the desire to offer fast service, the wrong word or response may slip in. That can lead to disaster.

Authors Kristin Anderson and Ron Zemke address this concept in their book, *Knock Your Socks Off Answers* (AMACOM). They've compiled a list of "Things You Should Never Say to a Customer":

"She's out of the state."

"Aren't you through yet?"

"It sure took you long enough!"

"You whine just like my in-laws."

"She went to buy another candy bar."

"Of course he has my number — I'm returning his call."

"He stepped out and took the newspaper with him."

"Aren't you the lady who called with that really dumb question?"

"If you'll start sounding like an adult and not a 2-year-old ..."

"Well, I never heard of anything like that before."

"Too bad. Better luck next time."

"I can't do that. Our policy is ..."

"Sir, that's just not possible."

"Yeah, well, so what?"

"You'll have to ... "

"It's not my job."

"I don't know."

"Little lady."

"Dude ..."

If you recognize yourself about to say any of these to a customer, bite your tongue before customers bite your head off!

QUICK TIPS

- **Downplay numbers.** Avoid bombarding customers with numbers and jargon, suggests *The Bank Teller's Handbook* (Probus Publishing). For example, don't say, "Hello, this is teller number 24 at branch number 7 of bank number 3-7 calling about check number 54432 on your account number 5543-60-5657." Instead try, "Hello, this is Ms. Jones from the Main Street branch of First National Bank. I wanted to ask you a question about a $50 check that you cashed at our bank this morning ..."

- **Monitor yourself.** Worried about speaking too quickly to phone customers? Monitor yourself by taping your calls. It's generally legal to do so as long as you are only recording your side of the conversation.

- **Save time and money.** When calling, let the switchboard operator know if the call is long distance. This may help you prevent long, costly waits on hold.

- **Customers prefer calls to letters.** In a recent article in *The New York Times*, Marcus Sieff, former chairman of Britain's largest retailing company, Marks & Spencer, said the company responds to customer complaints with an immediate phone call. Sieff said this personal and immediate approach is "more efficient and economical" than written responses and that customers like having their concerns addressed so rapidly.

- **Mark some faxes URGENT.** Use a thick black marker to write headlines like "IMPORTANT!" or "URGENT" on the top of your faxes when your previous attempts have gotten no response. These will get noticed! But use this technique sparingly. You don't want to be known as the fax sender who cried wolf!

- **Keep references close at hand.** Anticipate the information customers will call for most often. Then organize your work space to keep this information close at hand. Your customers will appreciate this quick response.

HOW EAGER ARE YOU TO OFFER SERVICE?

When you make a conscious effort to service customers *fast*, you send a lot of positive signals about you and your organization. One message customers pick up is: "I'm eager to serve you!"

There are several dynamic ways to convey an *eagerness* to serve. Take the following quiz to see how many you already incorporate in your day-to-day service to customers. Give yourself the indicated points for each YES answer, and a zero for each NO:

1. I make certain all my customers have my direct phone number. (10 points) _____

2. I have stayed past my shift to serve customers when they asked me to. (10 points) _____

3. I return calls from clients promptly. (10 points) _____

4. I've gone out in inclement weather to deliver parts and the like to customers. (10 points) _____

5. I take care of customers' complaints immediately and to their satisfaction. (10 points) _____

6. When customers want to see me before normal working hours, I always agree. (10 points) _____

7. I'm not against making or taking customer calls at home in extreme cases. (10 points) _____

8. I try to fulfill every reasonable customer request. (10 points) _____

9. I never ignore a customer call, even when I'm on a break, and I never ask that they call me back unless I'm on another call. (10 points) _____

10. I try to give all my customers every break I can, such as quantity discounts and free delivery. (10 points) _____

HOW HELPFUL ARE YOU?

Let's hope you scored at least 90 points on this "eagerness test." Customers like to give business to eager people, and, by your actions toward them, they can quickly perceive just how sincerely you want to serve their needs.

YOUR DAZZLE ME! TAKE AWAY

BE FAST

In the *Dazzle Me!* 7-Step Formula, Step 1 *isn't* just about quick action. *Anybody* can answer the phone, rush through a greeting, and manage some kind of solution … and break time records. Ironically, the fastest service also wastes more time than it saves because of all the additional phone calls and visits required to complete the business that was rushed in the first place.

In the *Dazzle Me!* Formula, speed is a state of mind. It means being conscious of both your time and the customer's time. It means giving customers the best service possible — because that's what they want — in the shortest amount of time.

WHAT YOU CAN DO *TODAY*

- **Rethink your greeting.** You should answer the phone with a friendly greeting and your name. But you can speed the call along by adding a phrase like, "How may I help you?" That can trim several seconds from your call time in a way that doesn't leave customers feeling short-changed.

- **Plan your calls.** Save time for you *and* your customers by planning the content of your call before you dial. That means taking a brief moment before you dial to "brief" yourself on the purpose of the call and to be sure you have all the information you need close at hand. Think of how much time it saves you when customers extend this courtesy; you can speed up your service by doing the same for those you call.

- **Slow? Say so.** If a customer has had to wait in line, or on hold, acknowledge that you appreciate his or her patience waiting. A simple "Thank you for your patience" can go a long way to ease the customer's stress.

- **Be fair.** When a number of customers are waiting their turn and you open a service line, don't allow customers to rush forward. Take the person who has been waiting the longest. Customers aren't so concerned about waiting a short time as they are about being treated fairly.

Chapter 5

THE *DAZZLE ME!* FORMULA
STEP 2: BE FRIENDLY

A smile costs nothing – and in the hospitality industry, it means everything.

— BRYAN D. LANGTON, CHAIRMAN AND CEO, HOLIDAY INN WORLDWIDE

INTRODUCTION

At the customer service training sessions he conducts for leading corporations, Stephen Broydrick deliberately saves the portion called <u>Attitude Makes the Difference</u> for the last hour of the program. But don't let that placement mislead you. "Actually, I save the most important for last," he explains. In fact, he says, a positive attitude is the factor that determines more than any other, a person's success and happiness in life. "Your attitude is your calling card," he explains. "It determines how the world treats you."

This is especially true in customer service, where so much of the impression your customers have of you and your organization is based on the attitude you project. "The person who arrives at work with positive expectations gets what she expects," says Broydrick. "So does the individual who antici- pates dealing with an endless string of impossible customers."

Broydrick says that those who get the most out of life – and advance the furthest in their careers – have one trait in common: "They're attitude leaders."

He explains, "Stephen Covey talks about how some people react to the weather, and how other people make their own weather. It's those who make their own weather that I think of as the atti- tude leaders."

Attitude leaders don't let a difficult cus- tomer ruin their day. They go to work expecting that it will be a good day. "The people who say yes to the challenges of the workplace are the ones who prepare for the workday and go the extra mile," he says. "They don't quit at the first sign of adversity. For them, a sense of satisfaction comes not from the easy days, but from sticking with it when an extra effort is required."

We aren't all lucky enough to be born with a positive outlook. But a positive attitude can be learned, Broydrick says. "You create a positive attitude by developing habits and then practicing those habits every single day," says the consultant. In the pages that follow, Stephen Broydrick shares his suggestions on how to develop a positive attitude. You'll also find additional ways to make sure you're dazzling your customers by consistently conveying a friendly, positive attitude that dazzles customers with the knowledge that you're happy for the opportunity to serve them.

WHAT WOULD YOU DO?

You deal with so many customers on any given day that it's hard to imagine having the time to give them personalized, friendly service. Friendliness sounds great, but who's got time?

THE DAZZLE ME! SOLUTION
HOW TO BE FRIENDLY FASTER

It's easy to fall into the trap of looking at customers as things on an assembly line, market research statistics, or account numbers — particularly if you deal with many customers daily.

How often have you, as a customer, dealt with cashiers who talk with each other but never to you? Or those who stick strictly to business, without even so much as casting a glance in your direction? Oddly, some people regard customers as just problems to get rid of, rather than as people to help.

But, it's people, not companies, who make the decisions to buy and provide repeat business, emphasizes Feargal Quinn, supermarket executive and author of *Crowning the Customer: How to Become Customer Driven* (Raphel Publishing). Even at the hectic pace with which you have to deal with customers, it is possible to take steps to offer them a more personalized level of service.

Quinn suggests some subtle, yet effective, ways to acknowledge customers as people:

- **Use their names.** Sound corny? Maybe, but it works. If you use a person's name, it shows at the very least that you've made some effort to do so. Suppose you handled a credit card or checking deposit. One glance at the name can make the compelling difference between, "Thank you, sir. Hope you'll come back soon," and "Thank you, Mr. Smith. Hope you'll come back soon." If you think about it, you probably have a number of opportunities to use customers' names.

- **Establish eye contact.** It's harder not to treat someone as a person if you actually look at them. As you first approach or encounter a customer, make establishing eye contact your responsibility. Why not throw a smile in for good measure?

- **Cast your customers in important roles.** That is, imagine that each person you serve is your best and most demanding customer (who has very high standards). If you do so, you'll have no problem motivating yourself to provide personalized service.

"These are tricks," says Quinn, "but they are not dishonest. They are simple techniques aimed at jerking your mind out of automatic pilot. They keep you from dealing with people in a one-dimensional way."

FORMULA FOR SUCCESS: TURN YOURSELF INTO AN ATTITUDE LEADER

In the introduction to this chapter, consultant Stephen Broydrick discussed how a positive attitude dazzles customers. He said that those who succeed the most in customer service and in life are what he calls "attitude leaders," reps who arrive at work with a positive attitude and share that attitude with their co-workers and customers.

Few people are *always* in a positive frame of mind. But in his book, *How May I Help You?* (IRWIN), Broydrick says that by following a simple three-step process, you can get the day off to a positive start. Here's his formula:

1. **Paint your day.** This is Broydrick's term for imagining positive outcomes for all your daily activities. First thing in the morning, set aside 20 minutes to stretch and feed your mind. Use those minutes for reading something positive, motivational or inspirational. Then turn off the light and close your eyes. "Utilizing a mental paintbrush, vividly imagine the events of a productive workday," he explains. "See the smiles of your co-workers and hear the thank you of customers and the healthy laughter in the break room or cafeteria. Imagine yourself resolving the problem of a difficult customer with poise and confidence." Painting your day allows you to take control of the first thoughts, images, and emotions of the day. "You'll find yourself carrying the benefits with you throughout the day," he promises.

2. **Have a plan for each day.** "On a piece of paper, list two or three goals you want to accomplish for the day," suggests Broydrick. "One might be to make one customer glad he called that day. Another might be to improve your relationship with the person who sits across from you. Let this be your roadmap for the day ahead."

"Time management courses advocate preparing a to-do list because it helps assure that important tasks are accomplished," says the author. "But having a plan does more than simply guarantee productivity. It helps you maintain a positive attitude."

3. **Act enthusiastically!** Imagine walking into the break room. A group of reps are sitting around a table complaining about customers. Are you inclined to join in the negative talk? Or will you try to convey something more positive and upbeat about your job and customers? "For whatever reason, your co-workers may not be strongly motivated to maintain a positive attitude. That makes creating and maintaining your positive attitude more challenging," says Broydrick.

Conveying a positive attitude creates a social risk because everyone wants to be part of the crowd. "I can always spot an attitude leader," says Broydrick. "It's that person who is willing to take the risk." Broydrick admits that it isn't easy to always feel positive and upbeat. "I say, '*Act* enthusiastically' because sometimes that's exactly what you have to do — act. But a positive attitude pays off. All other factors equal, it's your attitude that gets you the job, the raise, the date, the promotion, while others stand on the sideline. I'd say it's worth the effort."

DEVELOP AN ATTITUDE ACTION PLAN

To feel good about yourself and your job, you have to create personal performance goals for yourself — and stick to them.

"Hold yourself to a high standard," advises Tom Reilly, president of Sales Motivational Services. Reilly suggests developing a personal action plan that can help you keep focused on the standards you set for yourself regarding how you treat customers.

To set such goals, ask yourself this question: "What are a half-dozen things I can do to improve customer satisfaction?" Your list might include goals such as:

- Thanking the customer every time for his or her business.

- Smiling more often at the customer.

- Greeting the customer with enthusiasm to convey that he or she is a valuable asset.

- Never leaving the customer on hold for more than 30 seconds.

- Always asking if customer complaints can be relayed to management so that management knows what's happening.

- Offering a little extra to satisfy a dissatisfied customer.

- Listening in a nondefensive way to customer concerns.

Says Reilly: "I bet if you look back at those times in your life when you never felt more alive, more productive, or happier with the job you were doing, it was when you put forth maximum effort and held yourself to a high personal standard."

Your action plan can help get you there.

Attitude: Your Priceless Possession

The real difference between a positive and negative experience isn't about what you get out of it but, rather, what you put into it — your attitude. "Your attitude is your most priceless possession," said Mary Kay Beeby, of Crisp Custom Training in Seattle. At a Professional Secretaries International annual convention, Beeby cited several ways to improve your attitude, as originally listed in *Attitude*, by Elwood Chapman (Crisp). They are:

- **Look at the flipside.** Whenever something negative happens to you, try to think of the humorous or positive side of the situation.

- **Simplify! Simplify!** Think of three things you can do to make your life simpler. For example, learn how to use your computer to monitor your finances.

- **Insulate! Insulate!** In some situations, you have no control over the circumstances, but you can control how you react. Think of ways you can protect or insulate yourself from negativity such as practicing a hobby or talking to a friend.

- **Recognize the physical connection.** Your physical condition does have an effect on your mental condition. Just exercising 20 minutes a day, three times a week, can give you more energy. And exercise can be fun, such as rollerblading by a lake.

- **Write a mission statement.** Answer this question: If you had a year to live, what would you do during that year?

Service Sparkler

Are Customers Taking Up 'Too Much' Time?

Do you sometimes feel customers take up too much of your time? If so, your attitude needs some adjustment. Take some advice from Sandy Meyer, a customer service representative with McKey Perforating Company, Inc., in New Berlin, Wisconsin.

"When you feel people are using up your time, it changes your attitude toward them. You treat them differently and don't give them the best service possible," she says. "Instead of looking at how much time my customers *take* from me, I try to think about how much time I can *give* them. From that perspective, I'm thinking about how to give them more time, not less."

ADD 'A LITTLE SUGAR' TO EVERY CALL

Smiling and offering customers a friendly greeting goes a long way toward enhancing customer satisfaction. But if you *really* want to stand out from the crowd, you've got to do more. Try "adding a little sugar to every call," suggests Edweena Love, a customer service rep from Houston. "That means throwing in something a little extra special each time you talk to customers," says Love. "You want them left with a sweet taste in their memory long after the call is over."

How do you sweeten up your customer interactions? Here are some suggestions from Love and others. Of course, you won't want to try each idea on every call, but try to work one or two in whenever appropriate. You'll give callers something to remember, and that's likely to lead to customers who'll return!

To add a little sugar to your calls:

- **Address customers by name.** "I called a catalog company with a general question," recalls shopper Jim Denny. "The rep didn't need to know who I was to answer my question. But she asked my name and then used it a few times during the conversation. That struck me as a very sincere way of doing business."

- **Ask a personal question or two.** Not too personal, of course! But if you're talking with a longtime customer, try to refer to something he or she told you in the past.

    "It's not OK to comment, 'That dress you're ordering is a size larger than the one you ordered last year. Are you putting on some weight?' But it is OK to ask, 'Are you enjoying the fall weather?' or 'The last time we talked, you said that your grandson was coming to see you. Did he have a nice visit?' " says Denver-based telephone service representative Janis Zehl.

    "Our system has space for adding notes on each customer's account record," says Zehl. "Often, I ask a question or two for the specific purpose of obtaining information I can jot down and refer to the next time the customer calls."

- **Be polite.** Use the words "please" and "thank you" liberally. "Somebody once told me: 'You can never be too polite,'" says Peachtree, Georgia, phone rep Cindy Brinkole, "and I think that's true, especially when it comes to callers, because you really have so little time to leave a positive impression."

  Customer Alan Zaborowski says that callers notice when reps are courteous. "It only takes a few polite words to leave a good impression," he says.

- **Tell them something they don't know.** "I like to tell customers about some special sale we're having, especially when it includes something they normally buy," says service rep Barbara Levin, Chicago. "You're personalizing the conversation and telling them something that can save them money. They think of me as someone who's watching out for their best interests, which I am."

- **Compliment them!** This technique is Love's favorite. She lets customers know when she's particularly enjoyed talking with them or when they've brightened her day.

  But Love warns that compliments must be handled carefully: "I listen closely to find something I can say that is complimentary but true." It's worth the effort. "You feel good and the customer feels good because you've added a little sugar to the call," she says. "Everybody wins!"

Meet a Customer Service Dazzler

SAM CASCIO: 'ALL GUESTS ARE FAMOUS'

Does the name Sam Cascio ring a bell? Probably not. But this Chicago bellman, who has been on the job for well over half a century, has a simple, effective approach to good service — a good attitude.

When Cascio celebrated his 94th birthday recently, the Chicago news media turned the spotlight on the still-active hotel worker as the oldest bellman in the United States. He has been in the hotel business for 64 years, starting with the Steven's Hotel and continuing to stay on after it became the Chicago Hilton and Towers.

Cascio's positive attitude toward customer service has contributed to his longevity. When asked by the *Chicago Sun-Times* about the famous people he has served on the job, he replied, "All guests are famous to me. The guests are all nice if you treat them as the nicest. If you talk to them right, they'll all be nice. You don't walk away from a man who is cruel. You treat him nice."

TREAT CUSTOMERS LIKE GUESTS

Whenever customers visit your office or work area, play the role of gracious host and treat them as honored guests. That's a surefire way to build and nurture long-term business relationships, according to Randi Freidig, a professional speaker and trainer.

"As host, you'll assume responsibility for helping guests feel at ease and comfortable in your presence," Freidig observes. "He or she will feel at ease if you're comfortable with taking the initiative as host and guide throughout the meeting." She offers these suggestions:

- **Greet customers when they walk in.** Walk out to the reception area to welcome them personally. Then, be sure to lead the way back to your office or visiting area. "Don't just say, 'Go ahead, my office is the third door on the right,' and expect your guest to take the lead," Freidig cautions. "We've all experienced the embarrassment of going the wrong way or opening the wrong door in circumstances like that."

- **Help the visitor get settled in your space.** First, indicate where you want him or her to sit. "People who are sensitive to their positions as guests will be aware that it's not courteous to take up any space not offered by the host," Freidig says. Be very specific, so the visitor doesn't have to play awkward guessing games, such as "Where should I sit?" or "Where can I put my coat?" As the host, you should say, "Please have a seat," and then gesture to the chair where you want the guest to sit. Offer to hang up the visitor's coat.

- **Guide the business at hand.** As guests, most customers will look to you to dictate when to begin talking business. It's your job to be sensitive to the customer's mood. If he or she is chatting, don't cut off the conversation. Instead, look for a way to bridge small talk with business talk. Keep things moving along by introducing topics. For example, "You said over the phone you wanted to talk to me about our fall line. What, in particular, can I tell you?"

- **Walk the customer out.** "This is an extremely important part of the host's role," Freidig emphasizes. "I recall how embarrassed I was recently when I got hopelessly lost after a meeting with a client. I had to be guided back to the reception area by someone from the accounting department, where I'd ended up after several wrong turns. Put the finishing touch on your hospitality by making sure your guests leave feeling comfortable and well taken care of — and positive about you and your company."

DAZZLE 'EM MORE — WITH GOOD RAPPORT

Do you have a good rapport with customers on the phone? "Rapport can be loosely defined as a feeling of sameness. When we feel rapport with others, the channels are open, we're on the same wavelength," explains consultant George R. Walther, author of *Power Talking* (Berkley).

Without rapport, reps and customers are less likely to achieve their objectives. Rapport plays a major role in building customer satisfaction. The most basic methods of building rapport include using the customer's name during the conversation, and showing an interest in the customer's viewpoint.

But Walther identifies a second, more subtle route to gaining rapport — mirroring the other person's communication patterns. To make this type of rapport work, you first must understand that people think and express themselves in three different ways:

1. with visual images;

2. with feelings; and

3. with silent, internal "conversations."

Most people switch systems frequently, but one usually dominates, notes Walther. Picking up on a caller's style, and then mirroring it back to him or her, shows that you're both on the same wavelength. Suppose, for example, the person you are speaking with says, "As I look at this, I see lots of confusion. Perhaps you can shed some light on a few points."

To heighten your chances of being understood clearly and without resistance, you could respond, "Let's look at it from another angle and I'll see if I can create a clearer picture for you." "You wouldn't say, 'It sounds like you haven't heard what I'm talking about,'" Walther explains.

"To build rapport, match the representational system used," says Walther. "You do this by listening carefully and then 'packaging' what you want to express before it travels from your mind to your mouth to their ears. Target each caller's representational system and your statements will be more readily digested."

Walther says effective communication is the result of continuous monitoring and adjustment: "True communication is getting the response you seek. If you aren't getting the response you want, change, adapt, and model your behavior after those with whom you wish to communicate. You'll open the door of rapport more quickly and be able to communicate objective facts more clearly."

WHAT PERSONAL IMPACT DO YOU LEAVE WITH CUSTOMERS?

First impressions can be long lasting — whether or not they are accurate. It's smart, therefore, to concentrate on your personal impact on customers and make sure it's a positive one.

Your personal impact is created by a number of factors, some that may seem insignificant but, nonetheless, influence the customer. They include your speaking style, use of nonverbal body language, such as nodding to show interest, product knowledge, dress and personal grooming, and level of enthusiasm. When you present yourself positively and professionally, your customers will have more trust in your ability to serve their needs. The impression, in turn, can give you more confidence in your work.

Consult with your friends and colleagues about what kind of impact you have on customers. Honest feedback can direct you to areas that you need to improve. Then work to present yourself as a professional to the customer.

YOUR CHANCE TO SHINE

In a survey for St. Louis-based The Telephone Doctor, consumers told pollsters Fleishman-Hillard how courteous they think businesses are when handling customer calls. The results:

- **Excellent** — 25 percent
- **Good** — 35 percent
- **Fair** — 35 percent
- **Poor** — 5 percent.

There's good news in these numbers. With only one in four businesses earning a rating of "excellent," your business will stand out as one of the best if you make a point of always delivering a courteous, friendly greeting to customers.

PERFORM A '30-SECOND DETAIL CHECK'

Anyone who works with the public needs to be concerned with appearances. People will make snap judgments about your professionalism based on how you look. So get in the habit of doing periodic visual detail checks. They can save you from minor embarrassments such as mustard stains and missing buttons, notes Susan Bixler in *Professional Presence* (Berkley).

A quick inspection, she says, gives one confidence and frees up concentration for the customer. For example, have you ever been in a meeting and suddenly realized that you have food stuck between your teeth? You probably didn't hear the rest of what was said.

Customers deserve your full attention, so try Bixler's "30-second detail check":

- Check hair, teeth, makeup, earrings, etc. Straighten your tie or scarf.

- Inspect your clothes for stains and open or missing buttons.

- Button your jacket for a formal look; unbutton it for a casual look.

No, you shouldn't become obsessed with looking at yourself in the mirror every five minutes. But a quick check before a meeting or service shift will leave you feeling confident in your appearance.

Service Sparkler

HOW O.C. TANNER PERSONALIZES SERVICE

Customer service and sales representatives for O.C. Tanner have a unique way of introducing themselves to their clients. The Salt Lake City-based provider of employee recognition items faxes the introductions to clients serviced by its many regional offices.

In addition to a prominently placed photo of the rep, the fax lists the rep's responsibilities and customer service philosophy. The form displays the 800 number customers can call and lists the first names of the other reps in the regional office. To add a personal touch, the fax also includes such information as the rep's hobbies, favorite vacation spot, and favorite movie star.

NO BRAIN FOR NAMES? TRY THIS

One of the best ways to dazzle a customer is by referring to the customer or client by name. Customers are immediately impressed that you have made the effort to remember them. It makes them feel good to think that, with all the customers with whom you have contact, they were in some way memorable to you.

Those few seconds when you first hear the person's name are crucial to imprinting it on your brain. Most people think a poor memory keeps them from recalling names. But the real problem is that they are not concentrating and committing the name to memory when they first hear it. Use these steps to sharpen your recall:

1. **Look at the customer's face for an unusual feature.** "The idea is for your eyes to be drawn to this feature the next time you look at the person," says consultant and professional speaker Sam Deep.

2. **Listen — really listen — during introductions.** One reason some people have trouble remembering names is that during introductions, they are too busy focusing on what they will say in response. "Pay more attention to the other person's name than anything else being said," says Deep.

3. **Immediately translate the person's name into an object with a vivid mental image.** For example, Paul may become a ball and Karla may become a car. If the name can be used in a word association with the person, use that. For example: "Mr. Burns, red hair," or "Ms. Long, very tall."

4. **Repeat the person's name** as you acknowledge the introduction, "Hello, Mary."

5. **As you repeat the name, associate a distinguishing facial feature with the object you've picked for that person.** "The more absurd, animated, or vivid the association, the more likely you'll see the object — and recall the name — the next time you look at the face," says Deep.

6. **If possible, look back at the person a few times to reinforce the association with his or her face.** "This reinforcement will increase your powers of recollection," says Deep. "The more you do it, the more entrenched your mental image becomes, and the harder it will be to forget that person's name."

Don't try to remember every customer's name right away. Practice your skills on a few customers at first. As you grow more confident, you'll find it easier to use this technique on more customers.

MORE HELP WITH NAMES

All the positive benefits of remembering a customer's name will mean zilch if you don't pronounce the customer's name correctly. To be sure you're saying the name right, try these tips:

- If you go through a receptionist to reach a customer, ask for the correct pronunciation of the customer's name. Make a note in the file. For example: "Donald Phare: sounds like fair."

- If you contact a customer directly and are unsure of the last name, say so. Make your best attempt at pronouncing it, then add, "Please forgive me if I've mispronounced your name, but is that correct?" The customer will appreciate your consideration.

SERVICE — SIMPLY FOR THE JOY OF IT

In the mid-1960s, Ron McCann was working as a manager in his father's air conditioning repair company. Despite a record heat that summer, business was sluggish, and McCann couldn't understand why. Then one day he backed his car into his garage door. Inexplicably, that experience led McCann to a philosophy that has guided his business decisions ever since. Even he doesn't understand the connection himself. But that experience somehow sparked his discovery of "the joy of service," which he defines as "a combination of conflicting emotions — like pride and humility — that arise whenever you selflessly serve others."

McCann began teaching his new idea to employees at the air conditioning shop. Sure enough, business soon improved.

In *The Joy of Service!* (Service Information Source Publications), McCann "goes public" with his philosophy. Look for ways to implement his ideas into your own service strategy.

- **Serve for the joy of serving.** "Service isn't about making money," says the author. "It's about doing something you love because you love it, and getting paid for what you do because you've done it exceptionally well."

- **The joy in service comes from serving customers, not selling them.** It's a matter of attitude, says the author. "If you routinely ask yourself, 'Am I serving this person?' then you will always think of the customer and not of yourself ... If you (serve others) with the idea of making friends and helping people, then your life — and the customer's — will be enriched."

- **Put your personal signature on your service.** That is, take responsibility for your service. Imagine actually signing your name on the product you are selling, the auto you are repairing, the bank transaction you are completing, or the groceries you are bagging. "That commitment touches everyone who sees your work and your name. In a way, your personal signature is a declaration of your desire to give excellent service," explains the author.

QUICK TIPS

- **Give customers your name, too.** Besides using the customer's name, be sure to give the customer your name. It's not only friendly but also shows that you personally stand behind the promises you make with the customer.

- **Feel good? Show it!** Next time a customer or co-worker asks the obligatory, "How are you?" respond with a hearty "Great!" After all, a positive attitude is contagious!

- **They've had it with "have a nice day."** Sixty-one percent of customers don't like to be told "Have a nice day," according to a survey reported in *Voice Processing* magazine. The cheerful sentiment apparently has worn out its welcome. Next time, try simply thanking the customer for his or her call.

- **Avoid chatty voice mail.** Leave pleasant voice mail messages that include a short and friendly comment. But people are in a hurry when they listen to their messages, so keep the friendly messages short.

- **Put that smile in writing.** A handwritten note on a thank-you card can go a long way toward achieving customer satisfaction. Be sure to include information from the last telephone conversation, and always thank the customer for his or her business.

- **Use TV to improve your memory (really!).** Need help remembering customers' names? Memory can be improved by watching an hour of television and then recalling as much about the show as possible, says researcher Jean de Rotrou in *American Health* magazine.

QUIZ

LET YOUR ACTIONS 'KICK-START' A POSITIVE ATTITUDE

One of the messages of this chapter can be summed up in three words: Actions affect attitudes. No one wakes up each day feeling cheerful and upbeat. But when you're having a difficult day, the *actions* you take that *convey* a positive attitude will often help *kick-start* the frame of mind you are seeking. Here is an opportunity to see how you let actions point you toward a better attitude. Answer each question YES or NO:

	YES	NO
1. Do you arrive at work early enough (before customers call or appear) to plan your day's goals?	____	____
2. Do you answer each phone call with an enthusiastic and clearly spoken greeting?	____	____
3. Do you take the time to serve on special committees to help improve your company's service?	____	____
4. Do you look upon difficult customers as a challenging opportunity to provide more service or gain more sales?	____	____
5. Do you start each workday with a heartfelt "Good morning!" to your co-workers?	____	____
6. Are you always aware that, to each customer, you are the company?	____	____
7. Are you willing to make yourself a more valuable employee by spending some time each week learning about your organization's products and services?	____	____
8. Do you avoid those co-workers who spend their time talking negatively about their work and customers?	____	____
9. Do you make the effort to sound as if you are truly interested in helping customers?	____	____
10. Do you believe you can make a difference?	____	____
Total number of YES answers	____	

HOW POSITIVE IS YOUR ATTITUDE?

If you scored eight to 10 YES answers, congratulations! You regularly carry out the actions that convey a positive attitude about your work. If you scored less, remember that a good attitude in customer service not only will keep customers; it will also keep you in line for bigger and better things!

YOUR DAZZLE ME! TAKE AWAY

BE FRIENDLY

Friendliness isn't difficult. At some point in each day, even the grumpiest person in the world finds a moment to be friendly to another person.

But success in customer service depends not on a friendly, courteous moment here and there. Success comes in consistency. The challenge in the *Dazzle Me!* formula is in maintaining a positive attitude with every customer, every day. Anything short of that is a lost opportunity to provide the best service possible to your customers.

One way to achieve consistency is to periodically check your attitude. Train yourself to remember at various points in the day to ask yourself a series of questions. Those questions might include:

- Am I showing this customer how much I care?

- Am I being friendly?

- Am I conveying that I am interested?

- Am I making the effort to find out what's important to this customer?

- Am I looking for a way to add something special to this contact so it will truly stand out later in the customer's mind?

This "mini-mood audit" can help keep you on track. And that means giving more customers good reason to come back.

WHAT YOU CAN DO *TODAY*

- **Evaluate your friendliness quotient.** If you work on the phone, tape record your side of the calls. Make sure you record at different intervals of the day. Can you honestly say you're as friendly and upbeat with callers at the end of your shift as you are earlier in the day? If not, work to achieve a consistent level of friendliness throughout the day.

- **Use customers' names.** The easiest and quickest ways to increase your friendliness level is to begin using the customer's name while you are on the phone or sitting across from the customer. Everyone loves the sound of their own name, and the fact that you make an effort to recognize your customer by name will help you stand out.

- **Get into a positive mind-set.** Try various "tricks" that help you start your day in a positive frame of mind. You may enjoy reading for a few minutes before going to work, or listening to your favorite music at full blast on your car radio. Or you may like to start your day with an exercise routine. After trying out a few, settle on the one or two that are most effective for *you.* Your goal should be to start each day energized and ready to dazzle every customer (and co-worker) with whom you have contact.

- **Love what you're doing.** You aren't a robot. There are days you won't be in your most positive and upbeat mood. Those days require you to do a little acting. But be honest with yourself. If you find that you expend too much effort every day *trying* to sound happy and pleasant ... if you feel that your positive attitude is nothing but a false face you put on every day to get through your job ... then it's time to think about whether you truly belong in customer service. Dazzling customers is difficult, challenging work. Not everyone is cut out for the demands. Be fair to yourself — and your customers — and look for a new career.

Chapter 6

THE *DAZZLE ME!* FORMULA
STEP 3: BE FLEXIBLE

We've got to get back to a fundamental issue, and that is:

We all work first for the customer.

— LOUIS V. GERSTNER, JR., CHAIRMAN AND CEO, IBM CORPORATION

INTRODUCTION

If you want fewer customers, just be as inflexible as possible. Being inflexible means saying "no" as often as possible to customers. It means being surprised by anything that differs from the norm — an unusual request or question from a customer, an angry caller, or the accent of a non-English speaking customer.

Being flexible, on the other hand, means being adaptive. Today, there are fewer "typical" customers and fewer interactions that go strictly by the book. To survive as a service provider, you need to be open to change and willing to look at each customer's request with an open mind.

Being flexible is a form of self-empowerment. After all, it is easy to say no. But it takes effort and spirit to make decisions. If there is one lesson to be learned from the pages that follow, it is this: Don't become complacent. Take ownership of your customer interactions.

Learn what you can and cannot do within policy. When you're familiar with what can't be done, flip the equation: What does that mean that I _can_ do? You'll find that the job gets done much quicker when you make decisions without worrying, "What will my supervisor think if I don't consult with her?" Your flexibility will increase your customer loyalty because customers are drawn to those with an active interest in serving them.

On two occasions recently, customers complained to your supervisor that you had promised them refunds when, in fact, you had not. Can it be that you are not being very clear in your responses to customers? Or is it that some people simply don't take "no" for an answer?

THE *DAZZLE ME!* SOLUTION
AVOID MISUNDERSTANDINGS

Who wants to hear "no"? Not many of us. At times, customers may deliberately misrepresent what you've said so that they can get their way. But before you question your customers' motives, you should consider the possibility that the problem lies in a gap between what you're saying to customers and what they think they hear.

Consider this: You want to do everything you can to make customers happy. And telling a customer, "No, we can't do that," won't go over well. So, to soften the blow of "no," it's sometimes tempting to bend the truth so that "no" doesn't have quite so much sting.

The key is to say "no" to customers in a way that, although straightforward, is still sympathetic and reasonable. One three-step method is particularly helpful when such situations arise.

To avoid misunderstandings in the future, try these steps:

1. **Start by showing your concern.** Convey to the customer that you get no pleasure in having to say "no." You can say, "I'm sorry we cannot comply with your request ..."

2. **Next, say what you will do.** This phrase tells the customer that you want to help and conveys the specific actions you will take to get the problem resolved. The alternative may not be exactly what the customer wants, but it will usually help create an acceptable resolution to the problem.

3. **Finish by offering the customer ideas for action.** This conveys to the customer that he or she has some control over the outcome of the situation and that you consider the customer your partner in getting the problem resolved. This statement may involve recommending temporary fixes to the problem or actions that the customer can take to prevent

the occurrence from happening again. For example, suppose a customer tries to return merchandise for a refund without a receipt. After sincerely apologizing for being unable to offer a refund for the merchandise, you might say, "What I can do is allow you to exchange the merchandise for anything of equal value in the store. What you can do in the future is hold on to your receipts, so we can give you a full refund if this problem arises in the future."

By following these steps, you'll eliminate the chance for a misunderstanding. And customers will know that you want to do everything you can to make them happy.

MORE ABOUT "NO"

Although you may have to say "no" sometimes to a customer, there *are* ways you can cushion a negative response by using a friendly, approachable manner. And you can do so without misleading the customer. Consider this example:

Customer: *This is Tom Johnson. I sent you my video recorder two weeks ago. Did anyone there find out what went wrong?*

Phone Rep: *If you'll hold for a minute, Mr. Johnson, I'll check on it for you. (After a brief pause) I've got the report from our repair people right here. When did you say you purchased the machine?*

Customer: *Only a month ago. I expected it to work longer than that! The papers say it's guaranteed for one year.*

Phone Rep: *You're certainly right to expect more than one month's service. Our VCRs generally have an average life span of seven years before needing repairs. That's why we have such a generous guarantee and why we're proud to honor it.*

Customer: *That's what I thought — that is, until this happened. I assume you'll send me a new VCR immediately?*

Phone Rep: *Our repairperson took your machine apart, Mr. Johnson, and checked it out carefully. Apparently, it was damaged by something no manufacturer can guarantee against: a crayon. We make a great VCR, but no household equipment will hold up well with a foreign object stuck inside.*

Customer: *Now that you mention it, I stopped my little boy from jamming a pencil in it not long ago. He must have tried again. Does this mean you're not going to replace the VCR?*

Phone Rep: *I'm afraid our guarantee doesn't cover replacement of the machine in a situation like this.*

Customer: *I don't think I like that. But I really don't have a choice, do I? So, what am I supposed to do? We need to have a VCR that works!*

Phone Rep: *According to the service report, the damage can be repaired. Will you please hold for a minute while I find out exactly how much this repair will cost?*

Although the phone rep in this scenario had to say "no" to the customer, the call ended in a positive way. The rep refused the customer's demand for a replacement VCR without triggering further anger or hostility.

One reason the rep was successful is that she stuck to the facts. The machine was damaged under conditions not covered by the guarantee; therefore, the company couldn't replace or repair it for free. The call also ended successfully because the rep went on to suggest a solution: that the customer pay to have the machine repaired. She then offered helpful advice about how much the repair would cost.

You can tell customers "no" and turn the potential loss of a customer into a continuing relationship by being firm and tactful, and showing a willingness to help.

CUSTOMERS LIKE FLEXIBLE REPS

Flexibility ranks high among the qualities customers like in sales and service reps. That's the finding of a poll by Prudential Real Estate Affiliates. The other top qualities customers appreciate include:

- **Honesty and trustworthiness.** Be truthful about your products and services.

- **Availability.** Make it easy for customers to reach you.

- **Pleasantness.** Be friendly, polite, tactful, and helpful.

- **Professionalism.** Exude confidence and an ability to answer any question.

- **Understanding.** Listen to their requirements, anticipate their needs, and take a personal interest in your customers.

PACK A POSITIVE PUNCH

The telephone may be the most powerful tool in your organization. Yet, many telephone professionals unconsciously project negative impressions by using negative words and phrases. To put a more positive punch into your calls, emphasize the positive. A good rule of thumb: "Don't tell people what you can't do; tell them what you can do," say communications consultants Connie Brown Glaser and Barbara Steinberg Smalley in their book *More Power to You!* (Warner).

Here are some examples of commonly used negative telephone phrases. Read each one and judge what's negative about it. Then rephrase each statement in a positive manner and compare your opinion with the authors' "verdicts":

Negatively Speaking

1. Afternoon, Acme. Gail here.

2. I'm sorry. I can't help you. I work in sales. You should have called someone in our service department.

3. I'll be honest with you. I'm really not sure how long the warranty is.

4. I'll be happy to find that information for you, but I can't get it until tomorrow morning.

5. Sounds like we made a mistake. Let me transfer you to our manager of shipping. I'm sure he can help you resolve the problem.

6. I can understand why you're so upset, Mr. Jones, but please don't take it out on me.

7. I'm sorry to keep you waiting, but things have been crazy here all week.

8. I don't have that information. I'm just the receptionist.

9. We're short-staffed this month and can't ship your order until June 20. Will that do, or would you rather cancel?

10. You have to pay your current balance before you can order anything else.

Glaser and Smalley's Verdicts

1. Too informal. Try: Good afternoon, Acme. This is Gail. May I help you?

2. Who's sorry now? The customer! Especially since he has no idea who to call! Better: Joe Green, in our service department, has that information. Would you like me to transfer you, or may I have him call you back?

3. Customers don't appreciate this kind of honesty. If you're not sure of something, offer to find out. A better response would be: I don't have that information at my fingertips, but I can find out and call you back.

4. This statement is positive for the most part; however, "but" adds a negative slant. Better: Use "and" instead of "but": I'll be happy to find that information for you, and I can get it to you first thing tomorrow morning.

5. Again, almost positive. Replacing "problem" with "issue" makes it 100 percent effective. Try: Sounds like we made a mistake. Let me transfer you to our manager of shipping. I'm sure he can help you resolve the issue.

6. It's better to avoid words like "upset." Show that you care and that you're listening. Try this: I can understand why you feel as you do, Mr. Jones. You're saying that ...

7. The first half is positive, but the second half is not. Instead, say: I'm sorry to keep you waiting. How may I help you?

8. Don't underestimate your importance. If you convey that you are 'just the receptionist,' that's how callers will treat you. Instead, say: I'm the receptionist and don't have that information. I'm sure Ms. Baxter can help you. Let me transfer you.

9. Never give a customer an open invitation to take business elsewhere. Better: We can ship your order promptly on June 20. Thank you for your business.

10. Reframe this response in a positive way. Try: Once you pay your current balance, we'll be able to fill your next order immediately.

WATCH YOUR WORDS

Is the glass half-full or half-empty? Sometimes it's not what you say, but how you say it that matters. In telephone customer service, being flexible in how you say something can make or break your customer contacts. Consider the following examples of statements to avoid with customers — and the suggestions on what to say instead:

- Don't say: "Your order should be shipped Friday." Do say: "Your order will be shipped on Friday, January 27." Statements like the first, which use the word "should," leave doubts about your own confidence in your service. That negative — and possibly confusing — impression can be alleviated simply by being specific.

- Don't say: "I don't know why your problem wasn't solved last time you called." Do say: "I'm sorry about this misunderstanding. Let me get some information from you and take care of this now." The first statement indirectly blames someone at your company and gives the impression that your organization suffers from poor communication. That's not good for business or morale. On the other hand, putting blame on the customer will just make him or her defensive. The alternative response is better because it promises prompt action, which is really what the customer is asking for.

- Don't say: "I'm sorry you had to hold so long. Now what do you want?" Do say: "I'm sorry you had to wait. Now, how can I help you?" Ideally, neither statement is necessary because you are not making customers wait very long. But when you must place customers on hold, statements like the first are likely to make callers angry. This only makes things worse, since they're probably already on edge from holding.

  Your best course of action is to acknowledge that they've been waiting and that you appreciate their patience. Then quickly show that you are eager to help.

- Don't say: "Your bill should be correct now." Do say: "Your bill is correct now." In the second statement, you are speaking with confidence that the customer's problem has been corrected. He or she need not worry that, come the first of the month, the statement will be incorrect again. The rep making the first statement may have corrected the problem as well, but the customer can't rest easy until the next bill arrives in the mail.

- Don't say: "I'm sorry to keep you holding so long. We just don't have enough reps to take all the calls." Do say: "I apologize for the delay. Normally, we are much speedier." If there is an internal problem — such as a shortage of personnel — there is nothing to be gained by broadcasting it to the public. In the second statement, the rep is apologizing but also pointing out to the customer that, as a rule, service is better.

  Start paying attention to your own responses and how others speak with you.

Service Sparkler

FIND A NEW WAY TO SOLVE AN OLD PROBLEM

Here's how Steve Bailey, a technical support/repair supervisor for Metrotech, Sunnyvale, California, found that having a flexible approach to customer service helped him solve a tough customer problem.

Problem: Metrotech is a company that services and repairs cable locator equipment. Bailey observed that the downtime from sending in equipment for repair was costing customers in man-hours and service.

Key challenge: Because of the downtime costs, providing a faster turnaround for repairs alone was not a good enough solution.

Solution strategy: Bailey convinced management to institute an equipment loaner program. "Now we offer a quicker turnaround time and provide an equivalent loaner unit for customers waiting on repairs."

Outcome: "Absolute customer satisfaction. Providing loaners is unheard of in this type of service/repair field."

Lesson: "We learned that no idea should be eliminated when you are trying to provide service to the customer."

Break Your Calling Time Traditions

If you're not attaining the level of success you'd like in reaching customers on the phone, try being more flexible about when you call them. Work schedules are more flexible than ever, and it may be time to adjust your thinking about when the "best" time is for reaching those who make the buying decisions. Try these ideas:

- **Start earlier each day.** Some telephone salespeople spend a lot of time reading the newspaper and having their morning coffee before they make their first calls. Their logic? Prospects aren't in the mood to buy first thing in the morning, so why even try? But, in fact, one of the best times to get a prospect's attention is early, while he or she is alone and free from distractions.

- **Call during the lunch hour.** Many telephone salespeople don't bother making calls during the lunch hour. They assume their prospects are away from the office for lunch. Don't make that mistake. Many decision makers eat lunch at their desks. They find that there are fewer distractions and they can get some work done while they eat. Call between 11:30 a.m. and 1:30 p.m. You may have to translate what the prospect is saying between bites of her BLT, but it may be worthwhile.

- **Try calling late.** Many prospects also work late, when it's quieter. This is another good time for some uninterrupted selling. A prospect who is winding down after an eventful day may be in a receptive mood.

These suggestions should be just a starting point. The idea is to try to break the mold and free yourself from some of the habits you've made for yourself.

Meet a Customer Service Dazzler

MICHAEL MURPHY: 'IT WAS THE RIGHT THING TO DO'

When Michael Murphy was working as a customer service rep for Besche Oil in Waldorf, Maryland, in the summer of 1995, the area was suffering a major heat wave. And many of Murphy's customers needed emergency service on their air conditioning units.

Despite near around-the-clock hours from all the service reps, customers had to wait an average of seven to 10 days for service. When a 79-year old widow who lived in a trailer and was recuperating from broken ribs called for service, Murphy couldn't stand the thought of her being without relief from the 100-degree heat. So he retrieved a used air conditioner and an extra fan from his home, and installed them for the woman at no charge.

"I didn't tell anyone at my company because this was something I did on my own time," he explains. "I didn't do it for the praise, but as a neighbor. It was the right thing to do."

Murphy was recognized as a 1996 Dartnell Customer Service Hero for his flexible approach to solving customer problems. How does Murphy recommend others achieve service excellence? Treat each customer as an individual, he says. Be honest, use common sense, and be sure your solutions address customers' unique needs.

FLEXIBILITY WINS CUSTOMERS

Picture this scene: You manage a restaurant. A couple walks in and asks if you'll honor a discount coupon that you ran in the Sunday paper. They have a problem. They left the coupon at home.

Which of the following would you be likely to say?

(a) "Why don't you go home and get it?"

(b) "You'll have to have the coupon. That's the whole purpose of the ad!"

(c) "No problem. Where would you like to sit?"

If you responded (b), like many restaurants would have, you're likely to offend the customers and risk losing their business. The (b) response enforces a rule, but at what expense?

If the manager in question had elected the generous response (c), the customers would have been grateful. They would have come back and would have recommended their friends do the same.

The manager confused "means" with "ends" when he insisted that the "whole purpose" of the ad was delivering the coupon to the restaurant. The actual purpose was to bring in customers which, in this scenario, it did. The end was accomplished, so why insist that all aspects of the means were executed?

It's almost always the wrong choice to insist that customers jump through hoops simply to buy something from us. Details that exist only for the vendor's benefit are more than irritating. They threaten goodwill and profitability.

SILENCE ALWAYS COMMUNICATES SOMETHING

You stand face-to-face with an aggravated customer, and you notice how warm and sweaty you suddenly feel. You pull uncomfortably at your collar, shuffle a bit, and wonder if you are the only one who can hear your heart pounding. Across a mile of counter, the customer glowers at you, but doesn't utter a single sound.

What is going on in the customer's mind? Should you say something to break the awkward silence? What should you say? Should you say anything at all? Time seems to be at an agonizing standstill. You get the feeling that the customer's silence is implying that you should say something, but you're not sure.

Many of us have had uncomfortable experiences with silence from co-workers, supervisors, and customers. Silence can be frightening because its meaning is ambiguous — and we often assume the worst.

The messages silence can send out are countless — and the misinterpretations of them varied. However, there's one thing you can be sure of — silence always means something. If you learn how to interpret and use silence in your job, you'll possess a powerful interpersonal tool. You will be able to read people more accurately and have more control over how other people read your silent messages.

The following suggestions are ways in which silence can be used to your advantage:

- **To add emphasis.** If a customer has made a statement followed by a period of silence, you can be fairly sure that what was said is important. Silence gives the listener time to assimilate what has been said. It can reinforce your messages, too.

- **To signal time for a response.** Once a customer has made a point, he or she might then remain silent. Take this as a cue that it is your turn to speak.

- **To give yourself and others time to think.** Many people make the mistake of fearing silence. They would rather fill it up with rambling, fumbling speech than make silence work for them. It lets you buy some time to prepare what you're going to say next. Think back on speakers you've heard at seminars or meetings. The ones who use silent pauses — rather than filling them with "um's" and "uh's" — tend to sound more professional and self-confident.

- **To protect or separate yourself.** Don't let others pressure you into saying something if you would rather not. For example, a good way to respond to a customer's affront is with attentive silence. It will keep you out of trouble and can spare hurt feelings. Customers will get the message that you are listening to every word. But, be aware that silence can also be interpreted as consent or agreement, so you might have to reinforce your silence with a verbal rebuttal to make your meaning clear. Once you finish, ask the other person to respond. Don't make the customer wonder whether it's his or her turn to talk.

- **To cool off.** One of the best reactions to an upsetting situation is to temporarily keep quiet. Silence used this way can prevent an angry exchange of words in the heat of the moment that you (and your company) would later regret. Unfortunately, words can't ever be taken back. But, if you wait a few moments, you get a chance to calm down and collect your thoughts.

Don't assume that if other people are silent, they have nothing to say. Quite the opposite may be true. Their silence may be speaking volumes.

DON'T HESITATE TO SAY 'I'M SORRY'

After a late-night flight from New York to Calgary, Alberta, businessman Mark Bambeck was looking forward to picking up his rental car and driving to his hotel for a few hours of rest before an early morning meeting. But when he arrived at the rental counter, he was told his reservation had been lost—and that he'd have to wait two hours for a car. "It was a hassle," Bambeck said later. "It meant staying at the airport a lot longer than I wanted, and it meant getting three hours of sleep instead of the five I was hoping for."

But Bambeck took a seat and waited. Two hours later, the car rental clerk handed the keys over to Bambeck and he was on his way.

But Bambeck was upset. "What bothered me was that at no time did anyone at the car rental agency acknowledge my feelings or the inconvenience being put on me. At no time in the two hours I sat there waiting did anyone bother to say so much as 'I'm sorry.'"

Unfortunately, Bambeck's experience is not uncommon. Cynthia Crossen writes in *The Wall Street Journal*: "In airports, hotels, restaurants, stores, and offices around the country, consumers complain that even when service people make flagrant mistakes, they simply refuse to say they're sorry. In some cases, the expression of quick and sincere regret could prevent a letter writing campaign, an insurance claim, or even a lawsuit." Still, "I'm sorry" is rare.

Chicago-area psychologist Tim O'Brien agrees. "Companies may have excellent procedures in place for returning merchandise and correcting problems for consumers," he says. "But they overlook a very important psychological need customers have — that is, to have their inconvenience acknowledged and to hear that the company they're dealing with is sorry."

Shopper Diana Martin recalls recently returning from the grocery store only to find that several items were not in the bags. "When I went back to the store, they were quick to give me the items," she says. "But not a peep about being sorry for my inconvenience — that their baggers were negligent and that I had to make a trip back to get items I had already paid for."

O'Brien says some customer service reps aren't comfortable taking responsibility for actions that they personally did not take. "Their attitude is, 'I didn't cause the problem. Why should I apologize?'" Reps "need to remember that in the customer's eyes, they are the company," O'Brien says. "They need to realize that the customer doesn't blame them personally for the problem. And when reps say they are sorry, they are in effect saying it is 'ABC Company that regrets you've been inconvenienced.'"

The next time you're handling a customer complaint or problem, think of the customer's feelings — don't just fix the customer's problem, let him or her know you're sorry.

LANGUAGE BARRIER? PATIENCE IS THE KEY!

One situation in which you need to display the most flexibility is when you are approached by a customer who doesn't speak English. When this occurs, the most important thing you can do is to think first and foremost about the customer's feelings. "Remember, it may be a difficult or uncomfortable situation for you, but it's twice as difficult for the customer," says consultant Sondra Thiederman, Ph.D. Thiederman, president of San Diego-based Cross-Cultural Communications and author of *Profiting in America's Mulicultural Marketplace* (Lexington Books), conducts training sessions and workshops for customer service reps and others who may have contact with clients who don't speak English.

Thiederman offers these tips for overcoming language barriers with customers:

- Invite the customer to speak more slowly. "Do everything you can to encourage relaxation and confidence," says Thiederman.

- Paraphrase what you believe the customer has said. Then ask, "Is that correct?"

- Allow the customer to spell troublesome words.

- Take it slow! Give the customer time to communicate.

To help the customer better understand you:

- Don't shout. Speak slowly and distinctly.

- Emphasize key words. Recap frequently and don't cover too much ground at once. Allow pauses in the conversation so that customers have time to absorb information.

- Avoid long sentences. Keep one thought to each sentence. Avoid technical words or jargon.

- Avoid vague modifiers, such as "scarcely," "barely," and "almost." Non-English speakers often can't understand these.

- Follow the customer's lead. "Notice the English words the customer uses and try using them to get your message across," Thiederman says.

- Be as concrete and specific as possible. "Do not use too many words and do not talk too much," says the consultant.

- Check to be sure you are being understood. Ask, "Did I explain that clearly?"

Don't shy away from helping customers when there is a communications barrier. "The more contact you have with non-English-speaking people, the easier it becomes to understand them," says Thiederman. "Just don't pretend you understand when you don't. Be yourself, but be your most courteous and gracious self. That can overcome any communication barrier."

EMPOWERED REPS MANEUVER THROUGH COMPLAINT 'CAR WARS'

For most consumers, the automobile is the second largest purchase they may ever make (second only to their home). And they believe that after spending $15,000 or more for a new car, they shouldn't expect to experience any problems with it for many years to come.

When they do have a problem, they say so. Brooke Johnson, Chrysler's Customer Assistance Center service rep, is the recipient of many of those complaints — about 40 calls a day. She told Gannett News Service that her goals for each of those calls are (in this order) to defuse the anger, get the facts, and find a solution. "If you take it as a personal attack," she says, "you'll never make it."

Recently Johnson took a call from a Plymouth Sundance owner. In an exasperated tone, the caller explained how the car's molding had buckled in cold weather. The warranty had run out and the dealership would only agree to pay half of the $150 repair cost. "Why should I spend money to get it repaired?" the customer asked. "It wasn't done right the first time."

Johnson called the dealer, who said the car's owner damaged the door more by failing to bring in the vehicle for months. She then called the car owner back, who complained about the dealer's attitude. Johnson persuaded the dealer to repair the car free of charge one last time. "We give the customer the benefit of the doubt," she says. "He probably had damaged the door, but does it make sense to fight with him about it?"

This is the type of decision made hundreds of times a day at Chrysler's customer service center in Highland Park, Michigan; Ford's operation in downtown Detroit; and GM's Chevrolet facility in Troy, Michigan. Because service reps are empowered to make decisions normally left up to management, customers' problems are solved quicker and the customer endures less red tape.

Pam Clein handles customer calls on Lincoln cars at Ford. Clein gets calls that range from a simple warranty question to the angry customer ready to do battle. Active listening is the skill she finds most valuable. "If they're angry, I let them get that out first," she says. "When they define the problem, that's when you suggest what action you can take."

For Chevrolet's Linda Billingsley, the negative experiences of dealing with angry customers are balanced by the rewarding moments. For example, she recently fielded a call from a woman in California whose two-year-old Chevy conversion van was stuck in the driveway with a dead battery. Billingsley called local dealerships, which referred her to a towing operation. Within 10 minutes, the phone rep had dispatched a tow truck — paid for by Chevrolet — to the van's location. "We're empowered to do what's necessary for the customer," says Billingsley. "And when it works, you feel pretty good."

If your organization doesn't give you this kind of empowerment, take it upon yourself to show what you can do. If you must go to management with a problem, have a solution already worked out. Your supervisors will soon see how productive you can be.

QUICK TIPS

- **Counter intimidators with calm.** When a customer tries to intimidate you, stay calm and ask, "What can we do to help?" You demonstrate to the bulldozer that yelling isn't the only way to get cooperation. Try hard to get an answer to your question, and keep your tone positive.

- **Don't give in to hurried customer's pressure.** Suppose a customer is in a hurry and says, "I need this taken care of *now!*" Don't be bullied into resolving the problem before you have obtained the information you need from other sources. Say "I'm sorry, but I will have to study this and get back to you." That's always better than promising more than you can deliver.

- **Keep perfection in perspective.** Zig Ziglar, the popular motivational speaker, says a secret to success is to "work for progress, not perfection" and to "make your cause bigger than your ego." As you strive for providing the ultimate experience for each customer, keep in mind that *getting there* is part of the pleasure.

- **Cover for your co-worker.** A caller has left a message with you for a co-worker. Now she calls back asking why the call hasn't been returned. If you don't know, the best answer gives an appropriate business reason and doesn't commit your co-worker. "Ms. Smith has been unexpectedly tied up with a project. I'll remind her you called and that you hope to talk with her soon."

- **Embrace the new.** Don't grouse about learning new things. View it as a challenge. How can it benefit your current work? How could it help you in the future?

- **Spend more time online.** One way to be flexible in your work and career is to become more familiar with the Internet. More than 75 percent of the businesses in a recent survey said they will be increasing their use of online services. That probably includes your organization.

QUIZ

CUSTOMER SERVICE IS NOT A PERFECT SCIENCE

Customer service isn't a science. People are unpredictable, so interactions with them can't always be put into a specific category to be dealt with in a specific way. If it's important to you to always do things the same way, you'll lose the flexibility you desperately need to be able to react to customers' individual personalities and circumstances. Take the following test to see if you display the flexibility you need to dazzle your unpredictable customers. Answer each question YES or NO.

	YES	NO
1. Do you get upset if things don't go how you think they should?	____	____
2. Do you often assume that you know what customers are going to say before they open their mouths?	____	____
3. Do you know what you think about a new idea before you hear all the details?	____	____
4. Do you believe in the old adage that if you want something done right, you have to do it yourself?	____	____
5. Do you rehash customer interactions in your mind, going over what you did wrong and what you could have done better?	____	____
6. Do you feel that you can never apologize enough for your mistakes?	____	____
7. Does your mood away from work depend significantly on how your workday went?	____	____
8. Are you compelled to tell co-workers how they could do their jobs better?	____	____
Total number of YES answers	____	

HOW FLEXIBLE ARE YOU?

Eight YES answers suggests you know how to adapt to each customer's unique needs and that you are not thrown for a loop when situations arise that don't go just the way you anticipated. Six is acceptable, but if you scored lower, you need to work on this key area of the *Dazzle Me!* formula. Keep in mind that customers are people and that the only consistency about human nature is its inconsistency! Be more open to meeting the unique needs of each situation.

YOUR DAZZLE ME! TAKE AWAY

BE FLEXIBLE

In the *Dazzle Me!* formula for success, flexible customer service reps display several important qualities: *Flexible* reps are ready for any situation that may come their way. If a customer has a special request, flexible reps know how to make policies work *for* customers, not against them. They know when it's OK to bend the rules — and how much. When they must say "no," they are able to explain why. And, they try to emphasize what they can do for customers, rather than what they cannot do. *Flexible* reps are quick on their feet. They can field tough, unexpected questions because they're prepared for the unexpected. They don't let unusual situations — like callers who don't speak English — throw them for a loop. *Flexible* reps can bend — and they won't break.

WHAT YOU CAN DO *TODAY*

- **Assume "yes."** The next time a customer makes a special request, don't jump to say no. Instead, ask yourself, "Is there any reason I can't do this for the customer?" Be in a mind-set that conveys that no is the exception, not the rule.

- **Explain your "no."** If a company policy or procedure makes it necessary for you to say no, be able to explain to the customer the reason his request is being turned down.

- **Influence change.** Every organization should periodically review its policies to determine whether they truly serve customers. Offer to lead a committee that reviews policies and recommended changes. That way, you'll always be more comfortable explaining the *why* behind policies you have to explain to customers.

- **Pay close attention to customer requests.** If you keep hearing the same request from different customers, consider it a sign that it's time to change a policy. For example, at one grocery store, a clerk was very well trained in saying, "I'm sorry, we can't do that" when customers asked about the possibility of purchasing just a half-loaf of fresh bread. Another clerk noticed several customers made that same request. She passed on those requests to her manager. The outcome: The manager asked the supplier to create a smaller loaf of bread for people who live alone.

Chapter 7

The *Dazzle Me!* Formula
Step 4: Be Focused and Unflappable

I try to treat every customer like I used to treat my grandmother. When she was alive, I just shut up, listened to her, and kept trying to give her what she asked for until I was successful. Because I loved her and had never won an argument with her, I didn't waste time worrying <u>why</u> she wanted me to dig the silver out from its basement hiding place to eat her oatmeal with, or why I must always put the dish soap in <u>before</u> I started filling the kitchen sink with hot water. I just did it her way, because she wanted me to.

— Rick Stewart, CEO, Frontier Cooperative Herbs

INTRODUCTION

Customer service work isn't for everyone. Hours are long, the pay could be better, and the demands are great. Only the most focused and unflappable reps can survive and thrive in this environment in which there are always more customers waiting to be helped and upset customers show no restraint in letting you know what they think of your organization.

Focused and _unflappable_. Those are two words that are likely to be used to distinguish _Dazzle Me!_ reps from all the rest. _Dazzle Me!_ reps simply don't let anything get in their way when it comes to serving their customers.

Consider the reps at Advanced Telemarketing Corp. (ATC). On a daily basis, they handle more than their share of emergencies. But one Monday, even they might have felt that they were in a little over their heads. That's when the underground tunnels of Chicago's downtown Loop flooded with water from the Chicago River. An hour into the workday, the fate of the 250,000 people who commute to downtown Chicago was in the hands of the ATC phone reps.

ATC was subcontracted by the local Regional Transit Authority to answer phone inquiries from Chicago's 500,000 bus and commuter train riders. ATC reps spend several months studying city and suburban maps and schedules and actually ride each of the major routes. Each day, ATC helps about 10,000 commuters with questions

like, "What bus do I take to Wrigley Field from Oak Park?" and "Does that bus run after 9 p.m.?"

They do have their share of emergencies. But no one was prepared for the disaster that struck that Monday morning. By 10 a.m., city officials were asking everyone to evacuate downtown Chicago — including the ATC reps, whose building was one of those flooded. In addition, 17 underground train stations were closed due to flooding.

That meant that at a time when commuters needed answers from ATC most, phone reps were unable to serve them. ATC officials moved quickly to open a temporary office in a suburb far from the flooding.

Despite the lack of public transportation, which many of the reps depended on, they all found their way to work at their makeshift office.

"There we were, 30 of us, in a small room with 30 phones constantly ringing," reports one rep. "It was noisy and crowded, but we were able to answer calls again less than 24 hours after being forced to shut down."

In a press conference held a few days after the flooding disaster, Chicago Mayor Richard Daley pointed out that the evacuation of downtown went smoothly. He thanked everyone who contributed to its success. Certainly, ATC reps are among those who deserve to be praised.

That's _Dazzle Me!_ service. How would your commitment to customers measure up against that standard?

Maybe you're just too friendly: A few customers try to strike up conversations with you about (yikes!) politics and religion.

THE *DAZZLE ME!* SOLUTION
CONTROVERSIAL TOPICS? TIME TO REDIRECT

Most people know politics and religion are off-limits in the workplace. "By mutual consent we avoid raising these subjects," says Kristin Anderson, co-author of *Knock Your Socks Off Answers* (AMACOM). "It's an unspoken social contract designed to smooth the waters of daily conversation, especially in work settings, where we generally don't feel free to express personal views. In your personal life, you may feel free to agree or disagree with others' opinions," says Anderson. "But on the job, when the focus is on serving customers, disagreeing is risky, and agreeing can land you in the middle of an extended conversation that is irrelevant to your service task."

So how can you find a way out when presented with comments and questions about religion, politics, or other "hot" topics? When the topic is religion, Anderson offers this advice: "For the sake of customer service, you can acknowledge the good intentions without acknowledging the religious view behind them or encouraging further conversation. Your goal is to close the discussion and redirect the conversation to an appropriate topic as quickly and as simply as possible," she says. For example, if a caller asks, "Are you saved?" you might respond with, "Thank you. How might I help you today?"

When the topic is politics, your answer should not agree, disagree, insult, or make an issue out of anything. "Just redirect the conversation and move on," suggests Anderson. For example, if a customer says, "I can't understand why anyone would have voted that clown into office, can you?" respond with, "That's politics. How may I help you today?"

Difficult issues and personally held values do have a place in life, but on the job, they only distract us from providing "knock your socks off" service, says Anderson.

'FAST-ON-YOUR-FEET' ANSWERS TO TOUGH QUESTIONS

To be focused and unflappable, *Dazzle Me!* customer service reps need to be quick on their feet. That means being able to answer tough questions from customers without missing a beat. One way that is possible is by being prepared for the unexpected. How? By writing out in advance some standard responses to tough questions that might come your way. By reaching for the cards (or having the responses memorized in advance), you can provide quick, appropriate responses.

Here are some minor problems that may arise and fast-on-your-feet responses that can keep you on top even when the most unexpected question comes your way:

Problem: *A caller hasn't given his name and declines to do so after your request.*

What to do: *Let the caller know why you need his name. Say, "Having your name would make it possible to ... ."*

Problem: *The customer's speech is garbled, and you simply do not understand what she just said.*

What to do: *You don't want to insult the customer for being inarticulate, so you must be particularly careful. Start by saying, "I'm having a hard time understanding you, Ms. Smith. Could you please speak more slowly?" If that doesn't work, say, "Let me be sure I heard you correctly. Were you saying that ...?" and then repeat what you think the caller said.*

Problem: *A co-worker begins talking to you, and you've become distracted, missing what your caller has just said.*

What to do: *Be honest. "I'm sorry, Mr. Jackson. I was distracted for a moment. Could you please repeat what you just said?" Or say, "I'm not sure I understand you clearly. Could you please restate your request?"*

Problem: *The caller isn't speaking loud enough.*

What to do: *Say "We don't have a great connection, Mrs. Brown. Could you speak a little more loudly?" Or say, "We've got some background noises here that make it hard for me to hear. Would you mind speaking a little louder?"*

Problem: *It's early morning, and the person the customer wants to talk to has not yet arrived.*

What to do: *Since it's early and your co-worker isn't expected in yet, you don't have to worry about covering for him or her. Tell the caller the truth: "Mr. Kaplan hasn't arrived yet. I'd be happy to tell him you called." Then find out if it is necessary for the caller to speak to Mr. Kaplan. Ask, "Is there something I can help you with?"*

Problem: *It's early afternoon and the customer asks for someone who has already left to attend to personal business.*

What to do: *Don't explain too much. Say "Mary Smith is not in this afternoon. I can take your message and see that she receives it first thing tomorrow morning."*

Problem: *Your boss wants you to screen her calls.*

What to do: *Ask callers, "May I tell Ms. Williams who's calling, please?" or say, "Ms. Williams is in a private conference at the moment. As soon as she's available, I'll see that she receives your message."*

Problem: *The caller asks for information that is available from another department but starts explaining the problem to you.*

What to do: *Say "Mrs. Stacy in our accounting department is the person who would be able to help you most effectively. I'd be happy to transfer your call." Or say, "Thank you for explaining your concern. Mrs. Stacy in our accounting department is better prepared to help you in that area. I'd be happy to transfer you."*

SOMETIMES 'I DON'T KNOW' IS OK

Does being focused and unflappable mean you have to *know* everything? No! You aren't superhuman. Customers will ask you questions for which you don't have an answer. A candid "I don't know" response is far superior to the alternative — making one up. Too often, people feel they should know, so they fake it. Then, either they provide inaccurate information, or the customer can see right through the illusion as the rep fumbles for a reply.

Most of the time, customers will accept the fact that you don't know something. They just want the information. So, when you admit that you don't know, add the word "but" and tell the customer what you will do to find out. For example, if you're asked the specifications of a certain product, answer with a positive "I don't know, but I'll call you back later this morning with those figures." Notice the commitment to get information to the customer as soon as possible.

You also can keep your poise by saying something like, "That's a new product, and I haven't committed the numbers to memory. May I call you back after lunch? I'll have them then." Or consider this: "I want to give you the specific figures; let me double-check them and call you back." But use this approach only when you actually have a rough idea of the numbers because the caller might say they don't have to be precise.

Whichever approach you use, say those three words — "I don't know" — without any tinge of embarrassment or lack of confidence. Then be absolutely sure you make a commitment to get the information for the caller.

Service Sparkler

'CLEAN SLATE' MAKES YOU UNFLAPPABLE

Want to be focused and unflappable for your next call? Try clearing the slate, suggests Lori McGeary, a customer service rep for Standard Federal Bank in Troy, Michigan. "After I am finished with a call, I try to imagine that I am erasing a blackboard and starting with a clean slate before taking my next call. This gives me a fresh and focused outlook for my next customer."

DAZZLE ME! Q&A: STEPHEN COSCIA
RESPONDING TO IRATE CUSTOMERS

Sometimes a crisis or emergency can be the springboard to finding creative customer solutions. Consider what happened to Stephen Coscia. The company he worked for launched a new product that turned out to be faulty. As manager of the customer service department, Coscia had to prepare his service reps to handle the inevitable influx of calls that would be coming in from angry customers. Coscia decided to put the lessons he's learned in his 13 years of experience in customer service management into a book, *Customer Service Over the Phone* (Flatiron Publishing, Inc.).

Q: **From the experience you had handling calls over a faulty product, what was the single biggest lesson you've learned about handling complaint calls?**

A: *I learned that the single biggest mistake reps can make is not to allow upset customers enough time to vent their frustration. Let's say you're speaking with an upset customer. He is venting his anger about a problem and all the inconveniences and embarrassment it has caused him. The customer is halfway through describing the problem, and you're ready to interrupt him because you've already heard this situation described by other customers, and you know how to resolve it. But you should never interrupt customers when they are venting. They need the time to get the frustration out of their system.*

Q: **What about customers who vent too much — and have begun using vulgar language? How do you keep yourself focused?**

A: *We've all run into those. I suggest saying, "I realize you are upset, and I want to help you. But I'm not in the habit of being spoken to in this fashion, nor do I conduct conversations with people who use that kind of language." If that doesn't work, try this: "I'm taking notes, Mr. Customer. Can you repeat what you just* *said?" The customer will usually repeat what he's just said — minus the vulgar words. Chances are, from that point on, he will control his language.*

Q: What do you say to customers when they are through venting their frustration?

A: When they're finished sounding off, an upset customer usually will pause to take a breath. When they do, say something that shows that you empathize with them. I have a repertoire of memorized phrases I use to connect with customers. This is important because if the customer is loud and upset, I am also usually a little shaken up. These memorized phrases give me a chance to recover my composure and work out a game plan for satisfying the customer.

I usually say, "I understand how frustrating it is when that happens. If that ever happened to me, I wouldn't like it either." Empathizing in this way reinforces your similarities, not your differences. You'll notice a change in the customer's attitude as he realizes you're an ally — not an adversary — and he'll be receptive to letting you serve him.

'CRANKY' CALLERS COST $$

How can you keep cool and unflappable with cranky customers who won't stop complaining? Give them a chance to vent, solve the problem, and then decide if such customers are wasting your time.

Your first effort should be to try to solve the problem and keep the customer, says Paul R. Timm, a member of Dartnell's *Effective Telephone Techniques* newsletter Editorial Advisory Board and author of *50 Powerful Ideas You Can Use to Keep Your Customers* (Career Press). Try the following steps:

- **Listen.** Rephrase the problem and give the customer time to clarify.

- **Establish the facts.** This tactic can reduce the customer's tendency to exaggerate or generalize incorrectly. If he says he "tried calling all day but, as usual, you tried to avoid me," establish the actual number of times called and when, says Timm.

- **Don't apologize.** Or, at least, try to resist the temptation before you know whether an apology is in order. A too-quick apology can cause a complainer to push for an unreasonable solution.

- **Ask the customer.** What's the customer's solution? "The most important thing is to ask the customer to put himself in your shoes," says Timm. "That defuses a lot of unhappy customers right off the bat."

"You can spend an enormous amount of time with a person who isn't reasonable," he continues. "At some point, it doesn't make sense to save the customer. Instead, you can cut them loose and let the customer eat up your competition's resources."

CUSTOMER COMPLAINTS? NO PROBLEM!

Keeping focused and unflappable while handling complaints is not always easy. The key is to develop a specific method for handling complaint calls. If you follow your prepared formula, it's easier to keep from getting distracted by your angry or complaining customer, says customer service consultant George Walther. Of course, you have to be flexible when necessary, but if you use the following five steps as your roadmap, you're less likely to lose course.

Most complaints can be addressed with some variation of the following five key steps.

1. Prepare.

- **Check your body posture.** Even when the customer has no visual contact with you, body language says plenty about your attitude. Uncrossed limbs and erect posture mean you are attentive and ready to listen to customers.

- **Have paper and pen close at hand.** Taking notes keeps you focused on the content of the message and serves as a good written record of the conversation.

- **Clear your mind.** Resist the tendency to slip into "automatic."

2. Listen rationally.

- **Listen without interrupting.** Even if a caller is complaining loudly, you'll need to hear everything he or she says. Don't allow other thoughts to prevent you from focusing on the customer's concern.

- **Provide feedback.** You don't have the advantages of face-to-face contact over the phone, so use phrases that show you're listening, such as "Yes," "I understand," and "What happened next?"

3. Establish rapport.

Your caller needs to know you're both on the same team. To do this:

- Use the customer's name during the conversation.

- Indicate you have taken notes. Say "I'm writing some notes so I'll understand exactly what happened."

- Ask questions to clarify your understanding.

4. Create the solution.

- **Ask what the customer wants.** Grant the request, if you can. If not, work out a solution you both agree on.

- **Speak in positives.** Don't say "We can't do anything until next Tuesday." Instead, say "I'd be happy to schedule a service call for Tuesday."

5. Confirm and close.

- **Review your agreement.** Say "I want to be sure we're both clear about what I'm going to do."

- **Then do it!** "It's absolutely imperative that you take precisely the action you've promised," says Walther. Without that, you'll lose all the credibility and confidence you've worked so hard to gain with your customers.

Meet a Customer Service Dazzler

ANDREW ESTRADA: KEEPING HIS COOL MAY HAVE SAVED A CUSTOMER'S LIFE

For Andrew Estrada, a parking attendant who greets visitors and regular monthly customers, collects payments, and performs routine upkeep at the municipal parking garage in Santa Ana, California, it might be easy to not really notice all the customers who come and go. But Estrada knows the value of listening to customers.

He also learned the importance of keeping focused and unflappable in a potentially life-threatening situation. Estrada listened attentively, for example, when an elderly gentleman drove up and, in a confused tone, began asking for directions. "He started asking for directions to some hospital," recalls Estrada. After asking him a few questions, Estrada discovered the man wanted to get to a hospital in *Kansas* — not a short cruise from southern California!

Noticing the man's increasingly confused state, Estrada obtained the man's car keys, and called the police. While he waited, Estrada kept the man calm and continued to help other customers. Once the police arrived, Estrada and the officer noticed a medical identification bracelet identifying the man as an Alzheimer's patient.

The man was returned to his family, and Estrada and the officer were awarded the 1995 Alzheimer's Association Safe Return Award. As a result of his experience, Andrew has become a volunteer in local Alzheimer's Association activities. Andrew also received an Honorable Mention in the Dartnell Customer Service Heroes competition in 1996.

Andrew was saddened to learn that the man he helped died a few months later. But he treasures a letter he received from the man's daughter, which said, in part: "In today's society, it is so nice to know that someone would notice a person in need of help and would call for help. You are a special and thoughtful person. Thanks for caring."

REMAIN UNFLAPPABLE DESPITE TELEPHONE REJECTIONS

Rejection. Nobody likes it, but the fear of rejection can cripple your ability to make sales calls. That's why remaining focused and unflappable is an important quality for reps in telephone sales work.

Telemarketing expert Art Sobczak says the secret to remaining unflappable is to "insulate" yourself from the "no's." The most important thing you can do is to accept the fact that you will hear "no."

"Then don't take it personally. Remember, it's an *idea* the prospect is rejecting, not you personally," he says in the audiocassette series *Ringing Up Sales* (Dartnell). "Treat each call as if it will be your largest sale ever. It just might be."

Although you'll hear more "no" than "yes" responses, remember "the thrill of victory lasts much longer than the temporary sting of 'no,'" says Sobczak. Another tip: When you're getting more than your share of "no's" for the day, "recall a period when things were going well for you," he suggests.

Service Sparkler

HONESTY TAKES LOOKING INTO

To be focused and unflappable, customer service reps need to demonstrate integrity and honesty. When you display those characteristics, you don't have to worry that you'll treat customers in an inconsistent manner. And you'll always be able to stand behind what you say to customers. Often, however, honesty takes more than saying what we know to be true. It takes effort and work. Sometimes, we need to seek out the truth.

Evelyn Batts, of Grandville, Michigan, makes honesty a cornerstone of her work.

"As a customer service rep in the medical department of an insurance company, honesty plays an important role," she explains.

"Subscribers call me to find out if certain procedures are covered under their medical insurance. If I told them yes, without being completely sure, and the claim ended up being rejected because it's not a contract benefit, then I have actually lied to that person and caused them to be responsible for a bill. If I'm unsure of an answer, I do one of three things: 1) read the benefit summary; 2) ask a co-worker or supervisor who knows the answer; 3) call the company that does the actual processing of the claim.

"I feel that being honest requires going to whatever lengths necessary to give people correct information. This protects the person's trust in me to give them honest answers to their questions. Ultimately, this reflects on the company as a whole."

HONESTY MEANS 'FESSING UP'

Focused and unflappable service reps take responsibility for their actions quickly. As a result, they earn the respect of their co-workers and their customers, according to Adam Corren, a customer service manager in Santa Clarita, California.

Here's what Corren has to say on the subject:

"Co-workers and customers respect honesty, and that means 'fessing up' when a mistake has been made. Although the process can be embarrassing and uncomfortable in the short run, in the long run problems can be avoided and relationships can prove more successful when we are honest about our mistakes.

"For example, about six months ago, I allowed a marketing campaign to expire prematurely in our computer system. It was a good size mistake that was going to require some significant time to fix.

"It was very embarrassing to inform all the interested parties of my mistake. I could have worded my explanation in a way that would have relieved me of some of the responsibility. But the best thing to do was just admit the mistake, inform everyone of how we were going to fix it, physically fix it, and put it behind us.

"People respect honesty. They also respect someone who takes responsibility for his or her own actions. Dealing with a mistake in such a manner allows those involved to take care of the problem in an efficient manner. It also fosters relationships in which all individuals will be more honest and open about future issues, concerns, and questions."

LET'S GET PERSONAL — *NOT!*

Are you married? Where do you live? Are you a blonde? It's the point in a phone call that every phone rep fears: that moment when a caller gets just a little bit too personal.

For phone reps, being friendly with callers can create a catch-22 situation. On the one hand, reps want to build rapport with their callers. Cheerful, friendly reps add personality to an organization. On the other hand, sometimes being a little friendly backfires — big time!

Here are some examples from phone reps we've spoken with (to protect the reps' identities, we have used only first names):

- Some callers, says Sheila, "start telling you personal stuff — stuff you really don't want to know. I had one woman start telling me about an operation she was going to have to remove the flab around her tummy. I was thinking, '*Please* stop!'"

- Kim says the biggest problem is when men misinterpret a female rep's friendliness. "If the caller's a man, you can't say anything or they think you're flirting and start asking all this personal stuff." One call stands out: "Our computers are usually slow. So while I was waiting for information with one customer, I said something casual like, 'Well, the weekend is almost here. Do you have any big plans?' Before I knew it, this guy was trying to get me to meet him for a weekend at a hotel!"

- Tom says it's a problem for male reps as well: "Women are always saying things like, 'Is there some lucky young lady in your life?'"

Does this mean it's better for reps to stick strictly to business and avoid saying anything friendly to callers?

Not at all, says communications expert Laurie Schloff, author of *Smart Speaking* (Henry Holt & Company). When callers take friendliness as their cue to become even more friendly, tactfully change the subject, suggests Schloff. Keep in mind that you don't have to answer a question just because someone asked it. "Your first obligation is to your own sense of dignity and comfort," she says.

If a question makes you uncomfortable, try one of these strategies to dodge the question without losing the goodwill of the caller:

- **Offer a polite refusal:** "I know a lot of people don't mind talking about that. I guess I'm just a little old-fashioned."

- **Try humor:** "I can't tell you all my secrets!"

- **Zero in on something personal:** "Even my husband doesn't know that!"

- **Confess embarrassment:** "I have to be honest — I feel rather embarrassed by your question."

- **Question the question:** "I really have to wonder why you would ask a question like that."

- **Put up a legal roadblock:** "I plead the Fifth Amendment: no self-incrimination!"

Using these gentle techniques, you can usually get the conversation back on track and still maintain a relationship with the customer.

Service Sparkler

THROW THE BOOK AT THIS CUSTOMER

Customer service rep Margaret Evans of Skokie, Illinois, deserves a cheer for remaining focused and unflappable during this strange encounter:

"The bookstore where I work has lots of tables and big stuffed chairs, where customers can sit and peruse books or magazines before they buy them. We're not supposed to say anything unless the customer looks like he or she is doing some damage to the merchandise.

"It never ceases to amaze me how some people take advantage of this liberal environment. I often see students doing their homework, taking notes from the books as though they were in the library. And one guy reads a chapter of a science fiction novel each day during his lunch hour; when he finishes one book, he starts on another. I've never seen him buy anything.

"But a customer one day really took the cake. I was working at the customer service desk when she approached me, holding a women's magazine.

"Handing it to me, she asked, 'Would you photocopy this article for me?' I politely told her we couldn't do that — that she'd have to purchase the magazine. She became indignant: 'But I don't want to buy the whole magazine for one article!' When I calmly suggested that she try the library, she made a huffing sound, turned around, and stormed out of the store."

AUTHORITY CHALLENGED? SHOW YOUR STUFF!

Woman's voice: Good afternoon, Zukosky Remodeling.

Male caller: I'd like to talk to someone about getting some work done in a family room.

Woman: I can help you with that. Exactly what kind of work do you need?

Caller: Ah, do you think I could speak to the boss? I'd like to get an estimate.

Woman: I am the boss. How can I help you?

Angry callers. Nonpaying customers. Customers who lie. Linda Seibert has heard from them all. And "though they're a hassle," she says, Seibert's found she can handle just about any difficult caller. But the callers she has "zero patience for" are those who give her less respect because she is a woman.

Seibert is president of Zukosky Remodeling, a small company she and her husband, Paul, run from their home in a suburb north of Chicago. "Paul and our crew of three are at job sites all day," she says. "I do everything else — give estimates, order materials, pay the bills, make collection calls."

Hardly a day goes by, Seibert says, that she doesn't encounter a customer who is reluctant to speak with her and can't imagine that a woman is in charge of a remodeling business. "And it's not just men," she says. "Yesterday a woman who had a complaint about some charges said to me, 'Honey, I know you're trying to help. But why don't you have the man in charge call me back?'"

"They always think a man must have a bigger vote in the business, so if they don't like what I have to say, they think they can make an appeal to him."

One way Seibert has tackled the problem is by using her maiden name: "I never refer to Paul as my husband. If I did, the customer would immediately have this image of a dutiful housewife taking messages for her busy husband, who's really in charge."

Seibert has learned a few other tricks she says may help others who find their authority challenged:

- **Sound confident.** When Seibert first began taking calls, "I came across as mousy and unsure. I had this idea that everybody who called knew more about remodeling than me." But she learned that "if you sound meek, you encourage customers not to take you seriously." Seibert forced herself to speak with more confidence and discovered that fewer people were questioning her authority.

- **Know your business.** Have substance behind your confident style. "If you don't know your stuff, a customer will want to talk to someone who does," she says. "That's true whether you're a man or a woman."

- **Demand respect at work.** "You have to be sure your efforts aren't being undermined by someone else," says Seibert. When customers corner her husband for information, he refers them to Seibert. "We have a united front," she says.

Similarly, reps who are having trouble with a customer shouldn't rush to pass the problem on to their supervisors. "Make sure the customer knows why you are qualified to answer the question," explains Seibert. "As a last resort, you might say 'Let me try to help you. If you aren't satisfied, I'll give your call to someone else.'"

Be patient. "The world may not be changing as fast as we'd like, but when we force callers to change the stereotype they have, we're doing our part," Seibert says.

QUICK TIPS

- **Watch your words.** Avoid lecturing customers when solving a problem or handling a complaint. You only make customers more angry with statements like, "You should have mailed that payment sooner" or "Are you sure it was mailed?" Focus on solutions — not on placing blame.

- **Use calming words.** Defuse tense situations by using positive, calming comments, suggests Warren Blanding of the Customer Service Institute, Silver Springs, Maryland. For example, "I'll be glad to ..."

- **Lower your pitch to sound more authoritative and credible.** A high-pitched voice conveys nervousness and lack of confidence, says business communications expert Dianna Booher. If you want to come across as focused and unflappable, "adopt low pitches that sound confident and competent."

- **Be ready for an emergency.** If an emergency occurred right now, would you know whom to call? Make sure everyone in your area has a list of emergency phone numbers, including building security, the police, and local hospitals.

- **Even your "no" should sound positive.** When you can't give a customer exactly what he or she wants, try to find a positive slant in telling him or her "no." Is there a special product or service you can offer? A special price?

- **Find creative ways to counter mistakes.** For example, a bank in the Midwest sends a bunch of flowers in a mug with the words, "We're sorry" and the bank logo printed on it to customers who have experienced bank errors. The "Boo Boo Bouquets" are such a popular recovery technique, customers have been know to jokingly say, "Please make a mistake!" so they'll receive one.

QUIZ

ANGRY CUSTOMERS REQUIRE ATTENTION

There are few times a customer service rep needs to keep more focused and unflappable than when confronted with an angry customer. How you handle an angry customer is one of the skills your boss — and your customers — will most closely judge you by. Take the following test to see how you deal with volatile customers. Circle the response that best represents how you feel:

1. If a customer hotly exclaims, "I want to talk to your manager!" I:
   a. Think, "Fine, let my manager deal with this person!"
   b. Try to calm the customer by asking if there's anything I can do to help.
   c. Say, "My manager won't be able to give you any additional information than I have."

2. If I answer the phone, only to hear an irate customer on the other end yelling at me, I:
   a. Say, "I won't help you until you stop yelling."
   b. "Accidentally" disconnect the caller.
   c. Apologize for any inconvenience and offer to help in any way.

3. I find that angry customers:
   a. Break my concentration.
   b. Ruin my day.
   c. Teach me something about myself.

4. If, during an interaction, it becomes apparent that my customer is becoming upset, I:
   a. Proceed with the business at hand.
   b. Stop and ask the customer what is wrong and what I can do to rectify the situation.
   c. Become upset myself.

5. I believe that unhappy customers:
   a. Are likely to share their experiences with others, thereby damaging my company's image.
   b. Aren't worth worrying about; they seldom come back anyway.
   c. Will probably forget the whole experience once they calm down.

HOW WELL DO YOU HANDLE THOSE IRATE CUSTOMERS?

The correct answers are: 1. b; 2. c; 3. c; 4. b; 5. a. Although some people do have bad attitudes, you can do a lot to improve them just by being sympathetic and listening. Keep your focus on understanding why they are upset. Put yourself in their shoes: how do *you* feel when you're the customer and something has gone wrong?

YOUR DAZZLE ME! TAKE AWAY

BE FOCUSED AND UNFLAPPABLE

Being focused and unflappable may be the qualities that most separate *Dazzle Me!* customer service reps from all the rest. With a talent for keeping calm with angry callers and an ability to handle any situation forced their way, these reps don't simply survive in the high-pressure environment of customer service — they thrive in it!

WHAT YOU CAN DO *TODAY*

- **Prepare some answers.** Think of one or two of the most difficult questions you are commonly asked — questions that involve quick-on-your-feet responses. On index cards, write one or two standard replies to each question. Pull out the cards as needed when a "surprise" question comes your way.

- **Do more listening.** The next time an angry or upset customer calls, take a few deep breaths while he or she sounds off. Then, instead of concentrating on your response, focus on listening intently. Get a sense of what is bothering the customer. Then respond to his or her emotions first: "I know it was very upsetting when ..." You'll come across as cooler and calmer under the strain of a tough call.

- **Look for stress relievers.** To keep in top form, you must unwind from the stress of difficult customers and tough days. Make time for some exercise and leisure activities. Take those breaks. Even the most powerful batteries wear down if they're not recharged.

Chapter 8

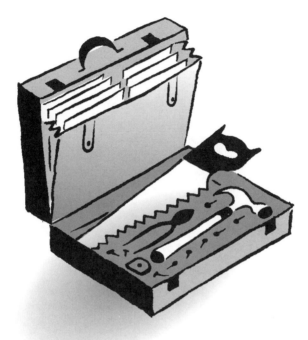

THE *DAZZLE ME!* FORMULA
STEP 5: BE A FIXER

The customer who is always right probably waits on himself.

— LAURENCE J. PETER, AUTHOR, *THE PETER PRINCIPLE*

INTRODUCTION

Let's be honest. No one likes it when customers call with a problem. Handling problems adds to a rep's workload. In addition, customers with problems are often angry, loud, and sometimes even abusive. But even though you might like to run the other way when a complaint call comes in, complainers are often your company's best friends.

Handling complaints and solving problems isn't only the right thing to do, it is also good for business, reports a study commissioned by the United States Office of Consumer Affairs and carried out by Technical Assistance Research Programs Institute (TARP).

The study found that:

● When minor ($1 to $5 losses) complaints were resolved to the consumer's satisfaction, 70 percent of the complainants reported that they would make purchases from the company in the future.

● When the complaints involved losses greater than $100, a similarly positive relationship between complaining and customer loyalty was found. Of those who complained and whose problems were resolved satisfactorily, 54 percent said they would buy from that company again.

This study suggests that those who have problems and make the effort to complain are customers who want to continue doing business with you and your company. Such customers recognize that problems are unusual. They may have had successful dealings in the past with your company. When a problem arises, they want to give you the opportunity to correct it so they can continue the positive relationship.

As this study suggests, handling complaints poorly negates all the <u>good</u> service you and your company have provided the customer in the past. But when you approach each complaint call with a "give it all you got" attitude, you'll be confirming to customers what they've already suspected: "I've had good reason to do business with this company. Sure, there was a problem. But WOW! did they impress me with the way they solved it!"

Drastic changes in your company's shipping policies have affected your customers. Standard shipping time has doubled, orders are often held to be grouped geographically, and shipments often go out a day later than shipping promises. Customer service talked to your boss who, in turn, talked to the shipping supervisor. Now, no one in shipping will speak to you. It's not only interfering with your job, but ruining your credibility with customers.

THE DAZZLE ME! SOLUTION
FIXING PROBLEMS BETWEEN CUSTOMER SERVICE AND SHIPPING DEPARTMENTS

Life could be a lot easier if solutions to every customer problem were simple. But, unfortunately, sometimes you're held back from offering customers the high level of service you want because of forces that appear outside your control — like how other people and other departments do their jobs.

In this scenario, it sounds like the company did a poor job of informing its customers about the changes in shipping policy. Since someone slipped up, you should take the initiative to inform your customers in writing about the changes and the reasons behind them. People can handle change much better if they know the reason for it. Make sure to run this letter by your supervisor and get approval first.

Next, address your own problem with the shipping personnel. You followed the proper channels when you went to your supervisor, so do so again. After you explain the situation, ask your supervisor to call a meeting with you, your colleagues in customer service, the shipping supervisor, and any shipping personnel you've had problems with. These two departments need to learn how to work as a team.

The purpose of this meeting should not be to point fingers of blame or to address personality problems. Instead, focus on how the two departments can work together to better serve the customer — that is the bottom line. Perhaps there are reasons why shipments have gone out late in the past that you don't know about. In turn, perhaps shipping doesn't realize how important it is to your relationships with your customers that shipments go out when you say they will. Explain it from your point of view. Certainly your colleagues in customer service have similar concerns.

If this meeting can remain customer-focused and solution-oriented, you may be able to get past the personality issues and create a working situation that you, your fellow reps, and your shipping department all can live with.

Think of That Complaint as a 'Gift'

A customer complaint is the perfect problem-solving opportunity — one that gives you a chance to secure that customer's loyalty for your company. Nurturing this loyalty begins with a positive initial response to the complaint, says Janelle Barlow, co-author of *A Complaint Is a Gift* (Berrett-Koehler).

"Research shows that customers have the most loyal relationships with companies that have helped them solve a problem," she explains. "A company is tested when something goes wrong. The customer is wondering, 'Are they going to be there to help me?' If you are, you win the customer's loyalty."

Before you begin solving the problem, Barlow says, you need to express appreciation for the complaint. "In our civilized society," she points out, "we thank people for a gift — even if we don't want it or have 16 others just like it."

Thanking a customer for a complaint "creates a feeling that you and he or she are in partnership against a common enemy," notes Barlow. The enemy is whatever the customer is complaining about. Otherwise, the customer links you — the service provider — with the problem. "You want to refashion this triangle," she says, "so that it's you and the customer against the problem, rather than the customer and his or her problem vs. you."

Barlow recommends expressing appreciation by saying something like, "Thank you for taking the trouble to tell us about this problem. We'll take care of it for you right now and do whatever we can to make sure it doesn't happen again."

Your unspoken message, she says, is "You've given us a gift — the opportunity to improve." Here are more tips for handling complaints during these touchy early stages:

- **Even when customers are wrong, thank them for their feedback.** For instance, if a customer misinterprets the instructions, never call attention to the error. Instead, simply say, "Thanks for letting me know. This gives me a chance to explain." Again, Barlow says, "There's an underlying message: 'You're a valued customer, and it's great you brought up this problem because now I can help you sort it out.'"

- **Apologize for the upset or inconvenience the customer has experienced.** "An apology really means something once you've received the customer's complaint as a gift by saying 'Thank you,'" Barlow points out. "He or she won't be so uptight about the problem, and you'll be more relaxed, too. You'll be able to come up with more creative solutions than you would if you were tense and worried."

Barlow notes that "some service reps wonder, 'If I apologize to the customer, does this mean I'm responsible for the problem, or that I'm saying the company is responsible?' No, it doesn't. To apologize is *not* to assume responsibility." She points out that "I'm sorry" is a phrase we use all the time.

PROBLEM SOLVING IN FIVE EASY STEPS

No doubt about it, fixing customer problems can be complex. But virtually every technique you utilize to help a customer is an outgrowth of five basic problem-solving steps. These five steps are the foundation, but what you do with them is what separates average reps from those who dazzle their customers.

Here are those five basic steps:

1. **Show empathy.** Let the customer know you are sorry he or she has experienced a problem. That doesn't mean you are saying that your company is necessarily at fault; you're simply recognizing that the customer has been inconvenienced and showing that you want to help in any way you can.

2. **Listen.** Remain neutral but listen to everything the customer has to say. Provide feedback; listening in silence makes the complainer think he or she is being ignored. Use words and phrases like "Yes," "What happened next?" and "I understand."

3. **Create a solution.** To find a solution, sometimes all you have to do is ask the customer what he or she would like you to do. Other times, you may need to offer a solution acceptable to both your company and the customer.

4. **Let the customer know what you intend to do.** Use positive words to explain what you intend to do to resolve the problem. Poor wording: "I can't do anything about this until Tuesday, when the service crew is in your area." Better: "I'd be happy to schedule a service call for Tuesday, if that is convenient for you."

5. **Confirm and close.** Review the agreement you've reached. Thank the customer for giving you an opportunity to solve the problem together. Then end the call.

Finally, be sure to follow through on any promises you've made. Especially valuable is calling the customer back to be sure everything is, in fact, resolved.

Meet a Customer Service Dazzler

NANCY BEHNKE: 'WHATEVER YOU HAVE TO DO, YOU JUST DO IT'

In customer service, there is a lot of talk of "going the extra mile." But when customer service rep Nancy Behnke personally transported a product more than 200 miles, she demonstrated that she will go many extra miles — literally — to help a customer in a pinch. It was that quality that resulted in her winning the 1st Place prize in Dartnell's first Customer Service Heroes competition.

Nancy has been a customer service rep for Dow Corning in Midland, Michigan, for 32 years. Her reputation for going all out for customers has led to her being the rep for some of the chemical company's biggest accounts. "The neat thing about Nancy," explains Robert B. Gamm, her team leader, "is that although she's been doing this for a long time, she consistently gives excellent customer service. She puts her customers first. She has an old-fashioned work ethic that you just don't find anymore."

Nancy was at home one Sunday when she received an urgent call from Avery-Dennison, one of Dow Corning's major accounts. A panic-stricken plant manager explained that if Avery didn't receive two drums of a particular paper-coater from Dow, the plant would have to shut down in eight hours.

Nancy called a Dow warehouse operator at home and asked that he go to the warehouse and prepare two drums of the material. She then called Dow's carrier and discovered that the delivery company would not be able to deliver the material by the 11 p.m. deadline. Despite numerous calls, Nancy was unable to secure a carrier for the material, in part because of a trucker's strike that was going on simultaneously. With all other avenues exhausted, Nancy took the matter into her own hands: After being assured that the materials were not hazardous, Nancy (accompanied by the warehouse operator) set out to personally deliver the material in her pickup truck.

"Nancy arrived just as the 'low on inventory' warning light was coming on at the plant," recalls Cindy Schiberl, a purchasing assistant at the Avery plant. "Thanks to Nancy, the plant did not have to be shut down. I think some of the warehouse people wanted to carry her around on their shoulders, they were so relieved."

After unloading the material, Nancy and the warehouse operator drove back the same night. Although they didn't get home until 2:30 a.m., both showed up at work on time the next morning.

In her characteristic modesty, Nancy says the personal delivery was no big thing. "You have to keep the customer running. Whatever you have to do, you just do it," she says. "You go the extra mile. That's what gives you a leading edge over the competition."

PUT CUSTOMERS BACK IN THE DRIVER'S SEAT

You're convinced: Some customers just enjoy being difficult. There's no other way to explain how they can get so much pleasure from complaining and arguing that they aren't even listening when you try to solve their problems. Why should you even bother?

Sometimes, in their anger and frustration, customers make it difficult for you to help them. But few customers actually enjoy doing battle. Most have legitimate problems that spark their anger.

"Remind yourself that angry customers probably have a need that isn't being met and believe you have the ability to start the problem on the way to being solved," says consultant Roberta Cava.

Cava is president of Cava Management Consulting Services. In *Difficult People* (Key Porter Books), she offers a helpful, two-step approach to handling those demanding customers:

Step No. 1: First, deal with the customer's feelings. "Use empathy to put yourself in the customer's shoes," says Cava. Say such things as, "I don't blame you for being upset. I'd feel that way, too, if it happened to me." Listen carefully throughout. Ask questions to clarify for yourself: "And then what happened?" or "Did the item you ordered not fit properly?" Let the customer know that you understand the problem and the cause of his or her anger. This will pave the way for the customer to clarify any points of confusion.

Step No. 2: Deal with the details. "Once you've dealt with customers' feelings," says Cava, "you're now ready to deal with their problems. Start by finding out what they want from you." Say something like, "I see we have a problem here. What would you like me to do that would help you?" Many customer service reps forget to ask this question, says Cava. "But it is a very powerful problem-solving tool." Often customers don't know exactly what they want from you. "You should then clarify exactly what is being requested and take steps to solve the problem," she says.

If, for whatever reason, you can't meet the customer's request, focus your comments on positive alternatives. "Tell the person what you can do that comes closest to meeting their need," says Cava.

If possible, give the customer at least two alternatives, but no more than three. Too many choices can cause more confusion. But offering more than one choice helps because "what you've done is return control of the situation to the client," says Cava. "In the customer's mind, he or she is back in the driver's seat."

THAT'S FUNNY — OR IS IT?

A little humor — used properly — can be a great tool for building rapport or defusing angry customers. Unfortunately, it's not always easy to tell which customers will be offended and which will laugh at a jest.

When Darrell Wilson made a joke on the phone to a customer about "higher prices for our favorite customers like you," his attempt at humor was met with complete silence. "It was a total miscalculation on my part," Wilson said later. "I wanted the joke to convey that, 'hey, you're a favorite customer of ours, so much so I can joke with you,' but it didn't come off that way. Obviously."

Jeffrey Messina is a customer service rep by day and a stand-up comedian by night. He says he gets more pleasure from his customer service work when he can inject some levity into his conversations with customers. "But entertaining an audience is different from serving customers," he says. "I know I can't bounce new material for my club act off my customers." Messina offers these tips on using humor with customers:

- **Humor usually is okay with customers you've had a good relationship with for a long time,** but be careful about being funny with customers who don't know you. "You may be able to get away with something light and generic with a new customer, but don't push the envelope," he says.

- **Be very careful about using humor over the phone.** "When a customer is standing there in front of you, you can judge a lot by his or her expressions and body language," says Messina. "But on the phone, the customer can't see your smile or other indications to know that you are joking. It's much more difficult to determine over the phone whether humor is appropriate."

- **When in doubt, don't joke.** "Humor can help, but humor that doesn't work is a disaster," says Messina. "Being a comic by nature, I sometimes have to do everything I can to control myself. But I'm always glad when I do because it's too easy for a joke to explode on you. The damage can be impossible to repair."

Service Sparkler

REP'S HUMOR ATTEMPT CARRIES SOME WEIGHT

Deb Geer used her quick wit to successfully calm an upset customer. Geer is a customer service rep for Weight Watchers in Clayton, Missouri. She received a call from a client who said that during a Weight Watchers-sponsored exercise class, a janitor at the facility started removing his clothes in front of the class.

"Nothing had happened," says Geer. "But the customer, understandably, was pretty upset. This could have evolved into a bad situation for us." Geer felt that a little humor would help ease the tension. She made a joke to the customer about whether the incident occurred "before or after" the janitor had been through a weight-control class himself. "There was a moment of silence — then the customer broke into a laugh," says Geer. "It's true that you have to be careful about how and when you use humor, but in this case, it worked."

Geer says humor helped in this situation in part because Geer then went on to take the customer's concern seriously. She apologized and explained that her organization would not allow an incident like that to happen again. She followed up by discussing the situation with the maintenance company that supplied the janitor, who was subsequently fired.

RESPECT CUSTOMER COMPLAINTS

Increasing numbers of customers are letting businesses know when they don't approve of products or services the companies offer, according to Kristin Anderson, author of *Knock Your Socks Off Answers* (AMACOM). Although clerks and service reps usually don't make company policy, most customers will sound off to them.

You'll impress customers by not simply nodding your head and listening to the customers gripe, says Anderson. She cites the example of a customer who complained to a convenience store clerk about the cigarettes and adult magazines sold there. The clerk replied, "I'm sorry you find those things offensive. If you'd like, here's a comment card to fill out. That way, we'll be better able to respond to your concerns. That card goes straight to the owner.

Thank you!" By saying he was sorry, the clerk showed respect for the customer's views. Also, he kept his own opinions to himself. Third, the clerk gave the customer an outlet to express her views in a way that could have some impact.

Anderson says the complaint did, in fact, produce results. The store owner moved the cigarette and magazine displays to less visible positions and promised to stop selling the products altogether if enough customers complained.

A FAIRY TALE

Sometimes going the extra mile to solve a problem simply doesn't pay off the way you expect! In fact, it's quite possible that your best efforts and persistence could be met with obstinate, and even nasty, resistance. Such times are the truest test of your devotion to service. Consider the following tale:

Ram works in the shoe department of a department store that puts a lot of emphasis on customer service. So when a customer left the shoes she had purchased behind in the store, he was only acting "in the line of duty" when he tracked down her home address and delivered them to her house.

A man answered the door with an unhappy look on his face. When Ram tried to explain why he was there, the man said, "I don't want to buy shoes," and slammed the door shut.

Ram rang the bell again. He explained again that he wasn't a shoe salesman, but that a customer at this address had left her new shoes at the store where he worked.

"My daughter don't want shoes either!" the man shouted. Again, the door closed.

Ram tried a third time. The older man opened the door, a look of anger on his face. "Unless you are the prince, Cinderella isn't interested in seeing you or your shoes!" Slam.

Frustrated, but smiling, Ram went back to the store and called, leaving a message on the answering machine for "Cinderella" to please come back to pick up the shoes she left at the store.

The grateful customer apologized for her father and told Ram, "My father's just impatient with door-to-door salesmen."

TURN TRICKY SITUATIONS AROUND

Dissatisfied customers come as no surprise to those who work in the service sector. That's what you're there for. But your initial response can turn a potentially troublesome situation to your advantage.

Dissatisfied customers can become satisfied customers who, in turn, continue to do business with you — and may recommend your company to others.

Here's how to turn around those touchy situations:

- **Attend to the problem quickly.** The longer customers wait for you to respond to a problem, the angrier and more impatient they become. If you attend to the customer's problem immediately, you save the sale and the customer.

- **Always see the customer's side.** Hearing complaints is never easy. But resist the urge to become defensive. Don't get upset or shift blame to the customer. Do your best to provide a remedy.

- **Dazzle 'em by going beyond the call of duty.** No job manual can allow for every contingency. But if customers are unhappy about a product or service, it's your responsibility to make things right. Find out what it takes to solve the problem — and keep the customer coming back.

- **Follow up.** Even if a problem has been settled, it's smart to ensure that it has by making a brief call or sending a short note of apology and explanation. Let your customer know you're genuinely and personally sorry for any inconvenience. Show that you work for a company that truly cares about its clients.

FIVE RULES FOR TOUGH TIMES

Fixing customer problems can be rewarding, but they can also take their toll. Keep these five suggestions in mind to help you through the tough times.

1. **The client isn't the enemy.** Be the customer's advocate at your company. Never say, "That's just how we do things here." Instead, work with the customers to fulfill their needs and solve their problems.

2. **Avoid treating customers as if problems are their fault.** We've all heard variations on "If you hadn't lost the charge receipt, you wouldn't have this problem." Determining blame usually makes the customer unhappy.

3. **Use fast phone service.** Returning a phone call may seem unimportant. But when you call a business, don't you expect instant attention? Follow the 24-hour rule: Return all calls within one day.

4. **In person, acknowledge customers quickly.** Don't wait for them to come to you. There's little as frustrating as being an ignored customer — especially if there's a problem. The customer may finally go away, but it will probably be for good.

5. **Work with customers as a team.** Even small spenders are entitled to your thoughtful attention. If payment is a problem, work within your company's policies to come to a mutually satisfying solution.

Service Sparkler

TOUGH PROBLEM? NO PROBLEM

You may handle dozens of calls each day and can probably handle most of them without sweating a bit. But occasionally a customer will present a problem that is anything but routine. When such problems arise, creative solutions are required — approaches that call for quick thinking and action on your part.

How do you respond to such customer problems? Here are two tough scenarios and how real reps tackled them:

Situation #1: Nonshipment from a vendor

Service rep: Cindy Larson, sales coordinator, Business Interiors Northwest, Seattle

Problem: Conference tables the customer had ordered were not shipped on schedule. Larson had promised they would be there in time for an important meeting. This left the client with no conferencing capabilities.

Key challenge: "I did not focus on uncovering the reasons for the nonshipment but instead on getting acceptable tables quickly. That was the priority."

Solution strategy: Larson did not inform the customer about the nonshipment until she had located replacement rental furniture. "That way, I was able to present him with a positive plan and not dwell on the nonshipment."

Outcome: The client appreciated the fact that Larson solved the problem before she called him. That spared him the added stress of wondering what to do.

Lesson: "You can't put the blame on anyone involved. You need to solve the problem and make it work."

Situation #2: Slow deliveries

Service rep: Theresa Anderson, Gerber Products, Fremont, Michigan

Problem: Kraft Foods, a customer of Gerber, was receiving orders five to nine days late.

Key challenge: Anderson's goal was to strengthen the buyer's trust and confidence in Gerber. She began by retracing all the steps that occur between the Gerber and Kraft warehouses to pinpoint where the delay was happening.

Solution strategy: "I determined that a carrier we were using was the source of the delays. I found a new one and convinced the buyer to accept the new carrier."

Outcome: Kraft now receives its orders on time. Also, in studying Kraft's account, Anderson discovered that this customer was in the wrong price bracket and eligible for lower prices. She reports: "They were very happy!"

Lesson: "Always listen actively to the customer. You can't correct a situation if you don't listen. Get the full details and follow up on what they're saying."

QUICK TIPS

- **Take that kid seriously.** Children don't always get the respect adults get, points out psychologist Elaine Rothstein. So, grab the opportunity: Treat the small fries with the same respect you give all your customers. You build a lifetime of goodwill.

- **Still holding?** A study found that customers will hold 40 to 44 seconds before they become impatient and hang up, but don't abuse their kind nature. One company that never makes customers wait more than 20 seconds found that that fewer than one percent of callers hung up.

- **Promise them anything?** There's a fine line between doing everything possible and promising more than you can deliver. Know policy so you never promise more than you can deliver.

- **Keep it to yourself.** You're working on a solution to a customer problem, but how can you be sure you can keep your promise? One way is to never promise anything that involves another person or a department. Make promises only for what you know *you* can do.

- **Don't point fingers.** There are times you'll be asked to solve a customer's problem that you didn't create. Don't isolate yourself from other employees by pointing the finger at one of them or at another department ("oh, those idiots in the mail room!"). Look at your co-workers as a team; each one is a spoke on a big wheel that couldn't turn without the others.

- **"Sorry, bye bye."** Even if a customer is about to slam down the phone or walk out of your office, try to leave an opening for a future change of heart. "I'm sorry we couldn't meet your needs, Mrs. Jackson, but I hope you'll give us another try in the future."

QUIZ

FUNDAMENTALS IMPROVE BATTING AVERAGE

After a day when everything seems to be going wrong, you may find it difficult to believe, but most customer complaints can be resolved. If you're going through a phase in which you can't seem to handle complaints in a satisfactory way, you may be skipping one or two fundamental steps in the problem-solving process. Take this quiz. It can help you determine whether you are covering all the bases.

	YES	NO
1. Do you first try asking customers, "What would you like us to do?"	____	____
2. Do you remain calm and courteous despite a customer's agitation?	____	____
3. Do you try to resolve the problem immediately, while the customer is still on the phone?	____	____
4. Do you convey urgency by using time-oriented statements, such as "right away," "immediately," and "within an hour"?	____	____
5. Do you identify yourself by name and emphasize your desire to solve the customer's problem?	____	____
6. Do you give callers an opportunity to "sound off" and let their grievances be heard?	____	____
7. Do you try to put yourself "in the customer's shoes" to understand how he or she feels?	____	____
8. Do you apologize for any inconvenience the customer has experienced?	____	____
9. Do you keep promises — carrying out the solution in the manner and time frame promised?	____	____
10. Do you thank customers for giving you the opportunity to solve their problems?	____	____

HOW DO YOU RATE WITH THE FUNDAMENTALS?

If you answered nine or 10 questions YES, keep up the good work. You're handling complaints and problems in a professional manner. If your score was lower, you aren't giving customers the attention they need and deserve.

YOUR DAZZLE ME! TAKE AWAY

BE A FIXER

Let's assume that *only* 2 percent of all customers during a given day experience a problem or are dissatisfied for some reason. Not bad, you say, considering the high volume of customers that do business each day. Before you come to any conclusion, let's do some arithmetic, courtesy of the Daniel Management Center of the University of South Carolina:

If there are 100,000 customers a day, 2 percent would add up to 2,000 dissatisfied customers. Multiply 2,000 by 5 (working days), and there will be 10,000 customers per week who are not satisfied. In the course of 50 weeks — almost a year — some 500,000 dissatisfied customers would be counted. Then, if each customer tells stories of bad service or bad products to nine other people, there would be 4.5 million negative stories out there about customers' experiences.

Preventing customers from having negative experiences is not always possible. However, being a "fixer" — someone who turns those experiences around by finding solutions — *is* possible. And you really show your mettle as a *Dazzle Me!* customer service rep when you make it your goal to fix every customer problem that comes your way, in a way that meets all your company's goals and requirements *and* makes that customer again one of the 98 percent of customers who are happy that day.

WHAT YOU CAN DO *TODAY*

- **Take every customer problem seriously.** Don't fall into the trap of starting to solve the customer's problem before he or she has a chance to voice it. You may have heard this problem 100 times this week, but it's a unique situation to the customer. He or she deserves your full attention. Keep in mind that *telling you* about the problem is a stage the customer must psychologically go through to begin putting the problem behind him.

- **But don't take it personally.** When a customer is screaming at you, it's natural to want to scream back, especially if you're not personally responsible for his or her gripes. But this will only make him or her more angry. Instead, remember that the customer's anger has nothing to do with you, but is a result of bottled-up frustration finally set free. You are simply the closest target. Put yourself in the role of psychologist; your immediate challenge is to help diffuse the customer's anger and to get him or her to calm down.

- **Know when to get help.** Whenever possible, attempt to fix customer problems yourself. But occasionally you'll come across a situation that you are unable to resolve without help. On these occasions, don't attempt a decision or make a promise the company can't keep. Discuss this issue with your manager and make sure you understand what kind of adjustments you have the authority to make. Even if you can't offer customers a solution in terms of money, goods, or services, you can at least listen sympathetically to their problems and make sure they are referred to someone who can help them.

Chapter 9

THE *DAZZLE ME!* FORMULA
STEP 6: FOLLOW UP! FOLLOW UP! FOLLOW UP!

A journalist told me recently, "You talk so much about customer satisfaction that you'd think Ford created it." I told him, "It's just the opposite; Ford didn't create customer satisfaction – customer satisfaction created Ford."

— LOUIS R. ROSS, VICE CHAIRMAN & CHIEF TECHNICAL OFFICER,
THE FORD MOTOR COMPANY

INTRODUCTION

"This is a routine, three-day job," suburban Chicago contractor Rick Hammell assured the customer, who put down a 50 percent deposit for the installation of a new garage door, automatic garage door opener, and short concrete driveway. But "routine" is hardly the word for what actually happened. A snafu in ordering the correct size door, the overcrowded schedule of the subcontractor hired to pour the concrete, and a spell of inclement weather combined to turn what should have been a short, simple job into a three-week ordeal.

Most customers would be angered by such a delay, but Rick's client kept calm. Why? Because Rick used several basic strategies for keeping the customer satisfied.

His strategies all revolve around <u>follow-up</u>, one of the key components of the <u>Dazzle Me!</u> formula for customer service success. Here is what Hammell did:

● He kept in touch. "I called the customer every day whether my crew was able to work or not. I wanted him to know that I had not disappeared, and his job was a top priority for me. I encouraged him to call me whenever he wanted an update. I instructed my answering service to page me immediately when the customer called. Even if I was out of town on another job, I called the customer back within 30 minutes."

● He didn't make excuses. "I was straightforward in explaining the delay, telling the customer precisely what the holdup was. Customers always appreciate honesty."

● He empathized. "I constantly assured the customer that I knew he was being inconvenienced."

● He accepted the blame – all of it. "Even though the basic delay was due to the subcontractors, I took full responsibility."

● He softened the blow by offering some extras. "I put up a temporary ramp so that the customer could put his car in the garage in the meantime. I substituted a better quality door than requested, and poured a longer driveway. I also replaced part of a sidewalk near the garage. Most important, I gave the customer a discount on the total price, to make up for the delay."

● He followed up some more. "I made it a point to be there to talk to the customer when the job was finally completed. That night, I called the customer to ask if he was satisfied with the work or needed any help operating the automatic door opener Two weeks later, I called again – just to check if things were still fine."

Hammell's experience shows how follow-up can help smooth a potentially difficult situation with a customer. On the pages that follow, we'll show you several more ways to utilize follow-up to create positive experiences for your customers.

WHAT WOULD YOU DO?

Talk about problems with follow-up! It's your company policy to respond to written complaints with a letter. But you've come across a letter that has gone unanswered for one month!

THE *DAZZLE ME!* SOLUTION
PHONE FIRST TO WIN THE CUSTOMER

In most cases, a written complaint merits a written response. But when a letter has gone unanswered too long, simple courtesy almost demands a telephone call. In this situation, you should check with your supervisor to see if you can make an exception to policy and call this customer. When you do, apologize for the delay.

Other times you might call a customer instead of writing:

- When you know you can help more quickly by speaking with the customer;

- When the customer is important or has been with the company a long time;

- When there could be a considerable public relations advantage in dealing with the matter by phone — or a real disadvantage in not doing so;

- When injury or a health hazard might be avoided by a quick response;

- When there is a high potential for legal action unless the complaint-handling process is swiftly put into action.

Bottom Line: Don't rush to answer every letter with a phone call. A customer may have written because he or she prefers to avoid the phone. A written response to a complaint provides you with a written record of the action you promised, should any question arise later. But do answer letters with phone calls when there is good reason.

Service Sparkler

'Call Roadrunner!'

It's difficult to follow up on the paperwork generated by one customer when the next customer is waiting to be helped. Toni Nieratko, a customer service rep for Mary Kay Inc., in Somerset, New Jersey, shares this suggestion:

"In order to take care of accumulated work throughout the day, we designate one person on a two-week time frame to research and take care of all the questions and problems that arise. When a problem comes in, a message is sent through the computer to the designated person, who has four to five hours daily to do nothing but handle research. This position rotates to each employee in the department, which makes for excellent cross-training. This individual is called our Roadrunner."

Follow Up Promptly to Requests for Company Literature

One of the ways you can send a positive image of your company to customers — and potential customers — is by promptly and efficiently handling their requests for printed information about your organization.

There are many types of information that callers request from companies. If it is not obvious to you what callers want, don't hesitate to ask them.

To fill requests effectively, you should first familiarize yourself with the publications at your company. Learn which ones are available for general distribution and which ones are intended for a specific type of request. For example, some companies provide a comprehensive prospectus and an in-depth annual report for potential investors and a separate summary of income and expenditures, written in layperson's terms, for the general public.

Sometimes companies offer a free brochure in their advertisements. Be sure you know about such an offer *before* the first request is called in so you don't look poorly informed to your callers.

Some publications, like annual reports, are expensive to produce, so you should be careful not to hand them out too freely. If a caller is really just interested in your most recent catalog, sending an annual report as well would simply be a waste of resources.

It's also a good idea to keep a tally of the requests you receive. Those numbers can be helpful when management is determining how many copies of a particular item to print. This tally might also reveal a need not currently being met. If enough people are asking for general information about products and services but no printed material exists, for example, management might consider producing such a piece to satisfy this high demand.

Another tip: Fill these requests as soon as they come in. You might keep a stack of large envelopes and a folder filled with frequently requested materials at your desk. Fill out the address as the caller gives it to you and put it right into the mail.

Providing information about your company to the public is a valuable and necessary service. Not only will you build goodwill, but you will also help generate new customers who may learn about your company from the materials you send.

DON'T LET THE SUN GO DOWN WITHOUT A SOLUTION

When the customer has a problem, don't let the sun set without doing *something* about it.

"If a problem can't be resolved on the spot, or before the sun goes down, you should *at least* set the process in motion and let the customer know that you're taking action," says Laura A. Liswood in *Serving Them Right* (Harper & Row).

It may only require making a phone call or writing a letter to reassure a customer that somebody's paying attention, says Liswood. But the important rule to follow is: Don't leave customers waiting.

MORTGAGE LENDER CALLS JUST TO SAY 'WELCOME'

Most home owners get a little jittery when they receive a call from their mortgage company. So it's only natural that customers of American Home Funding (AHF), a mortgage company, are a little suspicious and very much surprised when, during the early evening hours, their telephone rings and the voice on the other end of the line is a cheerful representative from the AHF home office in Richmond, Virginia.

"Some assume it's a sales call. Others think we're calling because we haven't received a payment," says customer service rep Polly Larimer. In fact, AHF representatives are simply calling customers to say "Hello" and "Welcome to AHF!"

The "New Customer Welcome Campaign" began when vice president Mike Stank enlisted volunteers who would be willing to stay after hours every other Tuesday for the sole purpose of phoning new customers. Currently, 16 AHF employees have volunteered to participate in the phone campaign. At first, the only volunteers were from the customer service department.

"A lot of people outside customer service are scared at the prospect of talking to customers," says supervisor Beverly Cassell. "Often, particularly when customers are calling you, it can be a negative experience because they're calling with a problem. But this is a positive experience. The customers think the calls are wonderful and they'll tell you so. We've had employees come up and ask for the assignment after they've talked to others who've done it."

Kim Martin was the first employee outside customer service to participate. "Someone who knew I like talking to people suggested I try it," she says. "So I did, and I loved it. The first night I had a ball. It's interesting to talk to different personalities and see how they respond."

The program has generated such positive feedback from customers and employees that it has been extended indefinitely. "People are just so overwhelmed that you're calling to welcome them," says volunteer Heidi Hess. "They think it's great."

While the welcoming crew has customers on the line, the reps confirm that the customers have received their payment coupon books. They also introduce the customers to other AHF services and answer questions. If the AHF caller can't answer a question, he or she makes sure that the customer receives a follow-up call the next day from someone who can.

The calls help AHF become aware of customer concerns before they develop into major problems. "Even though these are simple courtesy calls, they give us the chance to solve some people's problems," says customer service rep Carolyn Christian. "Sometimes, at the end of a long day, you don't want to go on the dialer," says Linda Gregory. "But these people are so receptive, you're glad you called."

FOLLOWING UP WHEN YOU'VE MADE A MISTAKE

On Monday morning, you realize you made a big blunder on Friday. You had promised a customer a delivery that cannot be met. You have two choices. You can conveniently "forget" what you had told the customer and hope the whole matter just disappears. After all, the mistake's been made and you can't correct it. Or you can take a deep breath, pick up the phone, and call the customer.

Obviously — we recommend the second choice! But we'd be the first to admit that calling a customer after you've made a mistake can be one of the most difficult forms of following up a rep must do. To make the call easier, plan ahead of time what you will say. These guidelines can help:

- Explain what happened.

- Apologize and accept the blame.

- Outline what can be done to rectify the problem.

- Send some tangible token of apology, such as a personal letter.

- Explain what steps you'll take to make sure the error doesn't happen again.

Your customers deserve your candid honesty. They may blow off steam, but they have a right to do so. But when that's done, they'll realize everyone makes mistakes, including themselves. And in the end you'll feel better for facing up to your mistake.

Service Sparkler

HARLEY-DAVIDSON REPS: DRIVEN TO PROVIDING TIMELY FOLLOW-UP

A customer places an order with you over the phone. You promise prompt delivery.

So far so good. But will that be your last contact with the customer until the customer receives his or her order?

Not if you work at Harley-Davidson Motor Co. in Milwaukee, Wisconsin.

Customer service rep Julie Hartmen says that loyal Harley-Davidson owners often are very anxious to get the parts they order for their motorcycles. So reps make a point of keeping customers informed about the status of their orders. "When you let them know you will 'watch' the order and inform them of the status, it makes the wait much easier for them," Hartmen explains.

"To do this, I keep a running list that contains the customers' names, phone numbers, and shipping data. When I have the information, I call the customer and indicate the item is on the way. It makes a world of difference to a 'patiently waiting' customer, and I always get a reply of 'I can't believe you really called me back — your company has the best customer service I've ever experienced!'"

FRIENDLY FOLLOW-UPS

After a customer has made a purchase, use post-sale follow-up to build goodwill, suggests Jerry Griffith in *Sell Like a Pro* (Dartnell). His suggestions:

- In a brief phone call, double-check that the order met the buyer's specifications;

- In a thank-you note, make suggestions about using what's been purchased;

- In a personal follow-up visit, convey the impression that you really care.

- In a "how-to-use" demonstration, train those who will be using the product.

FOLLOW UP ON A GOOD FIRST IMPRESSION —
WITH A STRONG *LAST* IMPRESSION

We hear a lot about making a good first impression on the telephone. But one can never underestimate the importance of the last impression, says Ron Willingham, a consultant for Integrity Training Systems. "People carry their feelings with them when they've finished talking with you," he says. "A good last impression will impact their desire to contact you again or refer you to their friends." One rule of thumb is to wait for the customer to hang up the phone. That way, you can never be accused of hanging up too quickly.

Here are some of Willingham's other suggestions for leaving callers with a good last impression:

- **Always thank the customer for calling.** It's obvious enough to thank customers when they place an order, but you should thank customers for contacting you, even if they called to complain.

- **Ask customers to call again.** Customers respond to genuine appreciation because it is so rare, says Willingham. "The salesperson or service rep who says, 'Thank you for choosing us, and please return soon,' makes a strong impact on customers," he observes.

- **Ask yourself, "How do I want customers to feel when they've hung up the phone?"** If an impartial person interviewed customers after they've talked with you, what would you want callers to say about you?

Write down the statement you'd like customers to make to that imaginary interviewer, suggests Willingham. "Having the statement posted near your phone can influence your actions and attitudes when you're speaking with your customers," he says. "Then every impression you make in the call — including your last — will make customers feel welcome, valued, and appreciated."

Service Sparkler

'KEEP IN TOUCH AND FOLLOW UP'

Here's how customer service rep Jeffrey Knight of Shop at Home, Knoxville, Tennessee, put *Dazzle Me!* follow-up skills into action:

Problem: A customer's order was way past due to be shipped. Knight had to do what was necessary to maintain the customer's faith in Shop at Home service.

Key challenge: "Locating the customer's order and tracking its progress throughout the shipping process."

Solution strategy: "To keep the customer informed, I called him every day and built a rapport."

Outcome: The customer received his order and loved it. He even sent Knight a thank-you card and has remained a valued client.

Lesson: "Keep in touch and follow up on things. Be honest with your client, regardless of whether the news is good or not so good!"

MAKE GREAT SERVICE A HABIT

If you routinely carry out the actions that provide great service to your customers, those actions will develop into habits. Then serving customers well will come naturally to you; in fact, it will go against your nature not to provide your customers with top-notch service.

In *Customer Service for Dummies* (IDG Books), Karen Leland and Keith Bailey, co-founders of Sterling Consulting Group, list several good habits customer service reps should adopt. Incorporate them into your daily routine and make high-quality service a habit:

- **Be on time.** "Being on time for appointments with your customers is a statement of respect," say Leland and Bailey. If you're unavoidably running behind schedule, call as soon as you know you are going to be late.

- **Follow up on promises.** "A major pet peeve for many customers is service providers who promise something and then don't follow through," say the authors. A prime example: A customer is told she will be notified as soon as her order comes in and then never receives a call from the company. "Customers are so unaccustomed to good follow-through that making it a habit scores you big points," explain Leland and Bailey.

- **Underpromise and overdeliver.** "The best approach is to promise only what you can be sure of — not what you hope will happen," say Leland and Bailey. For example, suppose a customer wants his new couch delivered by 3 p.m. You know that this delivery time is possible, but not guaranteed. "Promise delivery by 4 p.m. and you avoid disappointing the customer and delight him if the couch arrives earlier," suggest the authors.

- **Provide unique extras.** "By doing small, extra things for customers, your service is remembered and your company differentiates itself from its competitors," suggest Leland and Bailey.

- **Show empathy.** Empathy means understanding your customer's point of view, regardless of whether you agree with it. Some empathetic phrases to use are: "I understand why you feel that way," "I see your point of view," and "I hear what you're saying."

- **Treat customers as the most important part of your job.** With all the functions of a customer service rep's job — meetings, paperwork, and calls — it's easy to fall into the bad habit of thinking of customers as interruptions. "Focus on your customers as the reason why you do your job," suggest Leland and Bailey. "After all, ultimately they are the ones who write your paycheck."

- **Treat co-workers as customers.** There's a direct relationship between the quality of service you provide to your customers and the quality of relationships that you have with your co-workers. For example, if a customer calls asking for information that you do not have, you may need to contact another department. If the co-worker in that department is friendly and responsive to your needs, then you can get back to the customer faster and provide him or her with better service.

Meet a Customer Service Dazzler

Marie B. Stamper: 'The Satisfaction of Knowing I Made a Difference'

Some service reps go way beyond the call of duty when it comes to following up with customers. Consider Marie B. Stamper, the office manager for an ophthalmologist. She received 2nd Place honors as a Dartnell Customer Service Hero for going all out for her customers.

Here's just one example: A 56-year-old fisherman was losing his livelihood because progressive cataracts had caused legal blindness. He couldn't afford sight-restoring surgery, even though his doctor, Harold Christopher Ward, didn't charge him for it, because he could not cover other expenses involved.

That's when Stamper, office manager for Ward's Homosassa, Florida office, came to the rescue. "I started making phone calls and found assistance from state agencies, community groups, churches, and other places that most people don't know about." Groups like the Lions Club and Knights Templar helped, and Stamper got medications and post-surgical glasses donated. After surgery, the patient was able to return to work and support his family.

Stamper doesn't stop there. She consistently helps patients and nonpatients who have limited resources get help for not only eye problems, but other medical concerns. For example, Stamper gets free medication for people who couldn't afford it otherwise and shows them how to obtain it themselves. She has also uncovered sources for a multitude of resources such as crutches, braces, wheelchairs, insulin, transportation, and home assistance. She arranged for reconstructive surgery for a cancer patient and developed a network of medical providers to offer free care. The end results are a joint effort of people throughout the community working together, not just her, stresses Stamper.

Dr. Ward says she gives people hope and pulls off miracles, and she in turn credits him for giving her the time to offer special services. "I make a call here or write a letter there during nonbusy times," she explains. "I see it as a challenge to find an answer to every request I receive and, in helping, I've stockpiled a huge file of information. I'm teasingly called 'Information Central.'

"To me, this is a way of giving back," says Stamper. "I've been on the receiving end in the past, so I can empathize with what it's like to be in need. In fact, I have a good job now because I received help to get through college.

"The bottom line is really the pure satisfaction in knowing that I made a tiny difference," Stamper comments.

Collect Information from Customer Calls

Most follow-up is aimed at serving the customer. That is, when you follow up by checking the status of a delivery or follow up on a customer's question, you're helping the customer in a very direct way.

One type of follow-up is intended primarily to help *you* and your organization: the follow-up you do to get feedback from your customers. Feedback can help you evaluate how well you're doing your job and whether your company's policies and procedures meet and serve your customers' needs.

To obtain feedback, many companies carry out formal surveys. Such surveys can be time-consuming — and costly. And not always dependable. But why use such costly formal methods of research when there is a valuable resource right there? That resource: *you.*

How can you gather feedback from customers? Incoming *phone calls* and correspondence from customers provide a wealth of information. However, customer service professionals must not only receive but also *seek* information.

One excellent way to obtain feedback is actually very simple: by simply asking the customer for his or her opinions. If you're seeking an evaluation of you, as a service rep, you might say something like this to your customer: "I would like to make sure my work comes up to your expectations. Will you please tell me what you like or dislike about my work?"

Although your words may take customers by surprise because of their directness, you'll find that most people will quickly respond. Just as important, they may suggest how you or your company can improve the service. If you're interest in soliciting comments about your company, the following questions may be useful:

1. Is the product or service filling your needs?

2. What do you like about it or not like about it?

3. Do you see room for improvements? What might those be?

4. Does the product or service do what it was intended to do? Does it do more? If so, what?

5. Could it be designed better? If so, how?

6. Has it been reliable? Are you experiencing any problems? If so, what are they?

Customers like to be asked their opinions. It makes them feel involved and important. Most customers don't mind taking the extra time being surveyed, but you should first ask them if they wouldn't mind spending a few minutes answering some questions.

Next, decide what information is important. Record the information accurately and report what you learned to management. You are looking for trends. For example, if eight out of 10 customers tell you that the control lever on a product is difficult to depress, this is something your engineering department should know about. However, if only a few customers have told you about the difficulty with the lever, you may need more data. You can ask other customers who have purchased the model, "Have you found the control mechanisms to work satisfactorily?" When you have enough information, then you can pass it on.

Your informal surveys will go a long way toward keeping your company viable in the marketplace.

QUICK TIPS

- **Even with "no news," follow up.** Always call a customer back by the time you promised — even if it's to say that you don't have the information he or she wants and that you'll have to get back to him or her later. "Your credibility as a service provider hinges on how well you keep your promises," remind Karen Leland and Keith Bailey in *Customer Service for Dummies* (IDG).

- **Stop looking for blame.** When customers experience a problem, don't linger on who's to blame. "Accountability is important to remedy a problem so it doesn't happen again, but blaming is a waste of time," notes Tom Reilly, president of Sales Motivational Services in Chesterfield, Missouri. His advice: "Don't get defensive — get busy."

- **Follow-up should include future prevention.** OK, you've called a customer to check whether the solution you've put into motion worked. Good job. But your work is not complete. Effective follow-up also includes fixing the procedures that are causing problems to begin with. So if a delivery arrived late, find out what procedures aren't working, so future deliveries can be made on time.

- **Special attention faxes.** When you send a package to a customer, fax the tracking number of the airbill along with a copy of the express parcel shipping label. This assures the customer that the order is going out and provides all the information the customer needs if the shipment has to be traced.

- **Follow-up courtesy.** Courtesy is as important *after* your contact with the customer as it is when you have the customer on the phone or in front of you, suggests Ann Marie Sabath, president of At Ease Inc., a Cincinnati-based consulting firm. Sabath recommends always following up with thank-you notes to people who've made time to talk with you, even if the conversation didn't result in a sale.

QUIZ

ONGOING COMMUNICATION CRITICAL TO PROBLEM-SOLVING PROCESS

A key point of this chapter has been this: *There's more to handling a customer's problem than just correcting it.* Failure to follow up, for example, may very well negate the goodwill you've generated by handling the problem promptly and efficiently. The key is ongoing communication with the customer. The following quiz may offer you some insights into the many aspects involved in handling such situations. It is based on the First National Bank of Chicago's "10 Customer Service Commandments." Answer each question YES or NO, then check your score below.

	YES	NO
1. Do you call customers back when promised?	____	____
2. When a customer has experienced a problem, do you clearly explain the cause of the difficulty?	____	____
3. Do you make sure callers know the names and numbers of the people they should speak with about their problem?	____	____
4. Do you promptly let the customer know when a problem has been corrected?	____	____
5. Do you allow unhappy customers to speak to someone in authority when they ask?	____	____
6. Do you give customers an idea of how long it will take to resolve a problem?	____	____
7. Do you offer useful alternatives if the problem cannot be resolved exactly as the customer would like?	____	____
8. Do you treat customers like people — not numbers?	____	____
9. Do you tell customers how to avoid future problems?	____	____
10. Do you provide progress reports to the customer if the problem can't be solved immediately?	____	____

DO YOU KEEP THE LINES OF COMMUNICATION OPEN?

If you answered 10 questions YES, you're doing an excellent job in your follow-up communication with customers. Nine is average, but if you answered eight or fewer YES, you need to direct more attention to your customers' needs. Customers feel better about the outcome if you treat them like partners in the problem-solving process. That means keeping the lines of communication open.

YOUR DAZZLE ME! TAKE AWAY

FOLLOW UP! FOLLOW UP! FOLLOW UP!

Once you've agreed to help a customer, or to check out a complaint, your work has just begun. If you don't follow through as promised, everything you've accomplished to that point will have been wasted. Follow-up is a powerful *Dazzle Me!* tool in other ways as well. Calling loyal customers and thanking them for their ongoing business is a proactive use of follow-up. Following up by asking customers for feedback about the service you've provided is another. The bottom line is this: Your contact with your customers shouldn't be restricted to when they're making a purchase or calling with a problem. If you keep customers in mind — they'll keep you and your organization in mind, too. That's how loyalty is built.

WHAT YOU CAN DO *TODAY*

- **Provide special follow-up for at least one customer.** Customers appreciate thoughtful follow-up. Follow up on a special date (first order, anniversary of doing business, etc.). Or, follow up with helpful new information that specifically applies to those customers such as, "We now offer a 'movie package' that provides the same premier cable channels you've chosen, but at a lower monthly rate."

- **Make that call right now.** If there is bad news to report, don't put off telling your customer. Bad news is unfortunate, but there is no excuse for bad news that is delivered late.

- **Call with a status report.** Give at least one customer an update on the status of his or her order. Surprise your customer by assuring him "everything is on course" and he can expect that delivery the day it was promised.

- **Back up your promise.** If you promised to get a catalog out in this morning's mail, check to make sure it went out. If you promised to talk to the shipping department about getting an order out sooner, make sure you do it, and get back to the customer to let him know what happened. Remember, promises without follow-up are empty promises that will backfire on you. Don't force a customer to call your company again and again because you failed to follow up.

Chapter 10

THE *DAZZLE ME!* FORMULA
STEP 7: HAVE FUN!
(AND PUT YOUR STRESS TO REST)

When humor goes, there goes civilization.

— ERMA BOMBECK (1927–1996), AUTHOR AND COLUMNIST

INTRODUCTION

What characteristic do you look for most in your friends? Certainly near the top of most people's list would be: "A sense of humor." Everyone likes humor and the opportunity to enjoy a hearty laugh. Yet for some mysterious reason, many of us leave humor at the door when we come to work each day. "Most of us are far too serious," declares consultant Terry L. Paulson, Ph.D. "U.S. workers consume over 15 <u>tons</u> of aspirin a day. We move steadily through life with flat expressions on our faces. We've lost touch with the importance of fun in the workplace."

Human beings by nature are playful and spontaneous creatures. "We get 'professionally' serious and then pay comedians to do a job we've forgotten to do ourselves," muses Paulson. "Most of us were trained to put a lid on our humor, but we still tend to respect people who use it. People with a sense of humor are people you want to work with and listen to, and whose products we want to buy," he says.

Customers appreciate humor. Customer service is serious business, but a dash of humor can help resolve difficult situations — and help keep customers satisfied at the same time.

That's what happened when a customer came into a bank fuming over an error. As he approached the teller's window, however, he saw a small sign: "Mistakes made while you wait." The customer smiled, then chuckled. His anger dissipated, and he explained his problem

without rancor. The teller apologized for the problem and quickly corrected it.

Humor is good for you, too. "Dealing with customers successfully requires a high level of enthusiasm and confidence," write Humor at Work (Peachtree Publishers, Ltd.) co-authors Esther Blumenfeld and Lynne Alpern. "If you carry over negative feelings of rejection, frustration, or anger from one customer to the next, you will be significantly less effective." Therefore, they suggest: "let humor help you unwind. Take a few moments to look for the humor in your situation, put your aggravation in perspective, and create an optimum frame of mind for serving customers."

Need further convincing to have a good laugh? Read on. We'll show you ways to utilize humor at work, and we'll share additional stress-relieving tips and techniques.

WHAT WOULD YOU DO?

You tried using humor to calm a caller who was on hold a long time. ("Sorry! I shouldn't nap between calls!") It did not go over well.

THE *DAZZLE ME!* SOLUTION
WHEN HUMOR BACKFIRES

Humor isn't appropriate for every situation. "Don't be flip, and never be sarcastic," says Malcolm Kushner, a humor consultant for a number of companies and author of *The Light Touch* (Fireside/Simon & Schuster).

Humor works best when you know the customer and can anticipate his or her response. That's not always possible on the telephone. Apologize for your blunder, but keep it short. Say something like, "I'm sorry, I shouldn't joke. I know it's frustrating to be waiting such a long time." Then get back to business.

HOW TO BUILD STRESS RESILIENCE

In *Customer Service Over the Phone* (Flatiron Publishing), author Stephen Coscia, a customer service manager and trainer, offers additional helpful strategies for controlling stress when a customer is angry:

1. **Remember the rudiments.** "Your mother probably conducted your first and most important communication skills seminar when she taught you to say 'please' and 'thank you,'" says Coscia. "Believe it or not, those rudiments work. Unfortunately, when stress renders us ineffective, they are often the first things to go."

2. **Identify stress signals.** "Stress is that hyperactive feeling you have after closing a call with an upset customer, that tightening in the chest or feeling like you are out of breath," he says.

3. **Take slow, deep breaths.** "You have an unpleasant event that forced your metabolism to increase," says Coscia. "Breathing slowly will help offset the sudden change in your metabolic rate and allow you to remain courteous with your caller."

4. **Stop and think.** "Our society is very big on not thinking," says the author. "We are very big on doing. Thinking is secondary. Resist the urge to go on to the next call rather than to take a few moments to do a 10-second adjustment." Thinking about what

caused your stress will help ensure that you don't carry stress to your next call.

5. **Change your environment.** If necessary, take a break. "Short, five-minute readjustments will revitalize you so you can continue working effectively," says Coscia.

6. **Learn to forget.** "Don't replay bad experiences in your head," he says. "This only reduces your self-esteem and expends much-needed energy on an activity that yields absolutely no benefit."

7. **Wet your whistle.** Keep fruit juice or water nearby. "One of the results of the stress mechanism is a change in your voice," says Coscia. "It can become hoarse or raspy. Since your voice is your primary communication tool, ensure that it is always operating at peak performance."

8 **Don't blame customers, help them.** "Words can be weapons," he says. Use them in a positive way. If a customer makes a mistake, don't say, "You're wrong! It doesn't work that way." Instead, try: "I may be wrong, but I believe it operates a little differently. Please allow me to help." Says Coscia: "Let the words you use make you appear courteous rather than antagonistic."

9. **Use restraint.** With rude or abusive customers, use restraint instead of retaliation. "An angry customer's tone or behavior may be unpleasant," Coscia says, "but you should speak in a calm, consistent tone. This will help the customer conform to your professional behavior."

DAZZLE ME! Q&A: JOHN E. NEWMAN
KEEPING COOL — UNDER PRESSURE

Dreaming of the day you'll be free of stress? Forget about it.

"We will always have stressful problems to face, at every age and stage of our life, from cradle to grave," declares John E. Newman, Ph.D., an organizational psychologist and an expert in stress management and personal, managerial, and organizational effectiveness. The good news: "You can handle any stress that comes your way," Newman says, "if you have a plan."

That plan is the topic of Newman's book, *How to Stay Cool, Calm & Collected When the Pressure's On* (AMACOM). As president of Management Effectiveness Associates based in Yardley, Pennsylvania, Newman runs stress management workshops for such clients as Johnson & Johnson, DuPont, Merck, and Bristol-Myers Squibb.

Q: **In your book you talk about the "secret weapon" each person has for managing stress. What's that weapon?**

A: *The weapon is choice. We all have the power to make choices and to take action. We have the power to make conscious choices about the way we live our lives and the power to take action that supports those choices.*

Q: **But for a customer service rep who's in a very stressful situation — say her department is understaffed and everyone is overworked — short of quitting her job, which isn't realistic, she doesn't have a lot of control over her situation.**

A: *It's true, you can't always control what happens in your life. But you can control how you look at and respond to what happens to you. Therefore, you have some choice, if not in creating the event, then in how you look at it.*

The important thing to remember is that stress is not inherent in any situation. What makes it stressful is how you look at it, and that's something you can control.

Q: **Exactly how can a customer service rep control how he or she looks at a stressful situation at work?**

A: *Create a perception that is easier and more manageable for you. A rep can tell herself, "Yes, I'm being yelled at by an irate customer. But this is what my job is all about. I know they're going to be upset. I'm going to take pride in what I do. Instead of choosing to be hot, angry, fearful, negative, or unproductive, I can choose to be cool, calm, collected, positive, and productive." The result is, she will be able to go through life far more effectively, much healthier, and a whole lot happier. It's her choice.*

Q: **One of the points you make is that it's important to be in control of your own life.**

A: *You can make a major difference in your life. But to do so, you need to make a serious, deep-down choice about who you want to run your life — you or someone or something else. To gain control of your life, you need to start acting like an empowered individual. Learn to replace thoughts like, "That's life and there's nothing I can do about it" with "That's life and there is something I can do about it." Don't waste your time on negative thoughts, emotions, or actions.*

STRESSED? TRY THIS

Try these tips for handling workplace stress:

- **Conflicts with angry customers.** Joel E. Haber, a clinical psychologist in White Plains, New York, says the first step in handling angry callers is to separate your thoughts from your feelings. Tell the customer there's no need to yell without yelling back or getting personal. "Taking a step back or counting to 10 is a good way to cool things down," he says. Also, try not to take personally what difficult customers say.

- **Handling heavy workloads.** Negotiation can be an effective tool to deal with what you perceive to be an unfairly heavy workload. If, for example, a supervisor doubles your call quota, you have a right to ask if you've been assigned a fair load, says Jerry Lincoln, a clinical psychologist in Chicago. "Even if you don't prevail, just asserting yourself can reduce your level of stress," he says.

- **Losing perspective?** Consider the grand scheme of things. Ask yourself, "On a scale of one to 10, how close is this situation to life and death?" Use the answer to devote your emotional energy to the task at hand accordingly.

A DOSE OF HUMOR HELPS

One of the best ways to fight on-the-job stress is with a good laugh, says Dr. Joel Goodman, consultant and director of The HUMOR Project, Inc., in Saratoga Springs, New York. "Take your job seriously and yourself lightly. A difficult customer should be a 'red flag' that automatically says lighten up," says Goodman. He offers these tips:

1. **Tell yourself, "At least I'll get a good story out of this," and anticipate telling it.** Some companies have regular sessions in which service representatives share experiences and reward the best storyteller.

2. **Post a humorous quote in your work area.** You might also put a quote on a placard, change it weekly, and let customers see it.

3. **Anticipate conflict.** "Think of all the problems you might experience and, before they happen, have some 'Preparation — H' humor ready for your response," Goodman suggests. For example, if a customer has been waiting a long time for service, lightheartedly say, "Well, I guess you sure picked the wrong line today. I'm sorry for the wait." This can spark laughter and reduce friction in many instances.

4. **Enhance relationships.** Humorist Victor Borge once said, "A smile is the shortest distance between two people." Smiles help build relationships. "People often mirror what they see or sense," says Goodman. "If you smile, even on the phone, you increase the likelihood that customers will smile, too."

Another way to build relationships is by relating funny stories to customers. Inexpensive giveaways or funny props on your desk can be effective, too. One department store manager has a sign that reads "Sales Mangler" instead of "Sales Manager."

5. Increase creativity. "A 'Ha Ha!' helps you make an 'Aha!' connection by aiding you in stretching walls and barriers and making creative service breakthroughs," says Goodman.

Ask yourself how your favorite comedian would see a situation. Encourage a childlike perspective. "When handling a problem, ask yourself, 'How would an 8-year-old see this?'" says Goodman. "Your answers may not be appropriate to tell customers, but they can make you laugh internally and change your perspective."

6. Laugh with — not at — people. Use humor as a tool to build people up, rather than as a weapon to tear them down. Laughing at people creates adversarial relationships. Check humor against the "AT&T Test" by asking: "Is this humor appropriate, timely, and tasteful?" Unless you can answer "yes," don't use it.

"'You don't have to be a stand-up comedian, rattling off one-liners, to bring a humorous outlook to your job," says Goodman. "A simple smile or inviting lightness by asking customers to share their own humor can be major steps."

Service Sparkler

WHO-DUN-IT AT AT&T? THE HUMOR TEAM!

Everyone was getting just a little too serious around the New Jersey billing operations office, so AT&T associate manager Charlie Neagoy took matters into his own hands. He formed a humor team. "At AT&T, work teams are formed to tackle all sorts of problems," says Neagoy. "We weren't sure how management would feel about a humor team, but we've been pleasantly surprised."

The team, known as BOFFO (Billing Operations for Fun Organization), is made up of five members who meet regularly to develop innovative ways to inject fun and humor into their workplace. During its first six months, the team sponsored a pumpkin-carving contest and a white-water-rafting race. But its most popular event has been "Who Killed Bill?" — a murder mystery carried out over AT&T's e-mail system.

"We created a fictional story in which the top executive of the world's largest telecommunications company was killed off," says Neagoy. "We sent out clues every day over the e-mail system. The first three sleuths to correctly solve the murder won prizes."

The team earned an "Innovation Award" from management for the murder mystery. But what was most gratifying, says Neagoy, was "the number of employees who followed the clues and tried to solve the mystery. Even managers would stop us in the hall and tell us, 'We're behind this all the way.' They were having fun — and that's exactly what the humor team set out to accomplish."

So what are you waiting for? Form your own humor team and let the fun begin!

HOLD EVERYTHING! TIME FOR A CHUCKLE BREAK

- ***DOG DIALS 9-1-1.*** A dog in Nashua, New Hampshire, dialed 911 and saved her master's life. Lyric, an Irish setter, is owned by Judi Bayly, an emergency medical technician who must sleep wearing an oxygen mask to control her asthma. When Bayly's oxygen alarm went off one night, the first thing Lyric did was try to rouse her. When that failed, the dog did as she was trained: She knocked the phone receiver out of the cradle, punched the preprogrammed speed-dial button with her paw, and barked into the receiver. "Amazing," the dispatcher said. "Let's hope Lyric never learns how to dial 900 numbers."

- ***DON'T LET A LITTLE THING LIKE AN EARTHQUAKE SPOIL YOUR FUN.*** According to *Newsweek*, a Los Angeles deejay made the following announcement 30 minutes after an earthquake hit the area: "The telephone company is urging people to please not use the telephone unless it is absolutely necessary in order to keep the lines open for emergency personnel. We'll be right back after this break to give away a pair of Phil Collins concert tickets to caller number 95."

- ***AND YOU THINK YOU HAD A BAD DAY! HA!*** Midway through a Northwest Airlines flight from London to Minneapolis last year, 18 British passengers allegedly began cursing and throwing food when they were refused more liquor. One man hit a flight attendant. He was subdued by three wrestlers training for the U.S. Olympic team, who put him in handcuffs supplied by the pilot. He later was sentenced to 30 days in jail for the assault. The other unruly passengers were sent back to London.

CUSTOMER SERVICE REPS SHARE
'HAVING A TOUGH DAY' SURVIVAL TIPS

When you've just ended a call with a difficult customer, how do you bounce back so that you keep yourself focused for your next customer? Here are some ideas from Dartnell readers:

- **Oh, those letters never sent!** "Sometimes after a particularly exasperating call, I have difficulty shaking the bad mood I've gotten into as a result. So I take a piece of paper and write a note to the customer. Of course, I always destroy the note after I've written it.

    "For example, it might say, 'Dear Mrs. Jones: If you had let me get a word in edgewise, I could have solved your problem for you' or 'Dear Mr. Jones: When you yell at me like that, I want to clobber you!'

    "These are things I would never say to a customer! But by writing them down, then throwing them away, I have a safe outlet for my frustration. Plus, I have more patience during the call, because I know I can use this outlet if I have to." — *Connie Steinback, Echo Corp., Calabasas, California*

- **A walk on the calmer side.** "When I find myself having a bad day, I never go straight home after work. I go to the park or the mall just to walk around. I've found that if I go right home after a bad day, I take out my frustrations on my family. By going someplace else, I have time to relax and reflect on the events of the day. Usually within 30 to 45 minutes, my mood has changed and I'm able to go home and enjoy my family." — *Lynette Chambers, Owatonna, Minnesota*

- **Stress relief with a bang.** "My friend, who sits next to me, saved his noisemaker from New Year's Eve. Every once in a while, he blows it to relieve stress. We always laugh and everything goes back into perspective." — *Sue Hammond, Teaneck, New Jersey*

- **Hurry, pull out that file!** "Occasionally during the course of my career, I have received little cards and thank-you notes from customers who have taken the time to let me know that something I did was appreciated. I've made a little personal file with all these notes in it. When I am feeling a little discouraged, I just pull out this file and read a bit. It helps remind me that these customers make it all worthwhile!" — *Cristy Santopadre, Covington, Louisiana*

Thinking On Your Feet (Literally!)

As many phone reps know, "thinking on your feet" isn't just a figurative expression. Some people actually do think better when they get up out of their chairs and move around.

A common complaint among reps is that, because they're unable to see the person they're talking to, they can easily fall into the trap of lapsing into a monotonous, droning, and unenthusiastic voice. The next time this happens to you, stand up and get a different perspective. Don't be afraid to use non-verbals, such as head nods, hand motions, and even facial expressions, to articulate points. It doesn't matter that your caller can't see you. These gestures will help get your blood flowing and keep your enthusiasm high.

Desktop Stress Stoppers

Just sitting at your desk can be hazardous to your health, according to *Stress-Free Living*. The way you sit in your chair, hold the telephone, or work at your computer can lead to repetitive strain injuries, says Christin Grant, Ph.D., a research associate with the University of Michigan's Center for Ergonomics.

But you can prevent or reduce muscle strain and soreness from repetitive movements on the job, says Grant. Here are her tips:

- **Don't use your chin to hold the receiver against your shoulder when you talk on the telephone.** The strain on your neck muscles each time you do this builds through the day.

- **Sit up straight when working at your keyboard.** Don't slouch or hunch over. Monitor and correct your posture regularly.

- **Get up when you need to move around your office** rather than staying seated in your swivel chair and using your legs to "walk" yourself around.

- **Every 10 minutes take a 30-second break from tasks that require any type of repetitive movements.** Change your body position, straighten your posture, stand up, roll your shoulders, and flex your neck or fingers. All these movements relieve tense muscles and stimulate blood circulation.

- **Take "R & R" on schedule.** Don't make a habit of skipping coffee or lunch breaks in order to work straight through and get a job done faster. Your body, mind, and work will ultimately pay the price in pain, stress, and quality.

NIGHT SHIFT WOES

Many customer service reps are forced to routinely change shifts. Not handling the change with care can put added stress on your mind and body. It can take as long as one day per hour of time shift to become acclimated to a change in work schedules, according to Peter G. Hanson, M.D., author of *Stress for Success* (Ballantine Books). That means starting a two-week shift will result in up to eight days of decreased mental alertness, drowsiness, indigestion, and other possible ailments.

A worker can typically expect a substandard performance during the first week of a new shift, followed by a "good week." But if you then change back to your old shift, you can expect another bad first week while your body adjusts to yet another new routine.

If you're suffering from a changing schedule, you might want to see if your supervisor will consider longer (and fewer) periods for you to work the night shift. That can reduce some of the rollercoaster effects.

Hanson offers these specific suggestions for helping your body adjust to night shifts:

- **Sleep at the same time each day if possible.** "And don't be afraid to take a catnap before you start your shift if you were unable to take a long sleep during the day," he says. Even if you are allowed to nap at work, your body will benefit more if you are in the familiar confines of your own bed.

- **Install heavy curtains in your bedroom.** "Light can be a powerful weapon, alerting our chemical wake-up alarms," says Hanson. "Keep the shades drawn when you are sleeping during the day."

- **Trick your body with light.** "Use sunlight or room light to wake you up at home when you want to force yourself into a night-sleeping routine," he advises. Giving your work area extra light can help keep you alert.

- **Exercise to become alert.** Day or night, exercise can invigorate you and help offset a new schedule.

- **Listen to music.** Lively music can wake you; soothing music can help you sleep.

NOT ENOUGH SLEEP: EVERY REP'S NIGHTMARE

No one needs to tell you — you know you need more sleep! But how do you make time for the extra zzz's?

Margo Baron, a Phoenix, Arizona, sleep researcher, suggests this:

- Go to bed 15 minutes earlier tonight. Maintain that schedule for one week. Don't change the time you're waking up. Don't sleep in on the weekend.

- Next, add 15 minutes more for one week. Each week, add 15 more minutes until you find that you're waking up feeling fresh and awake. No matter how much sleep the experts recommend, the best gauge is how you feel when you wake up.

Baron says this system works. "Even though your body wants the additional sleep, you need to gradually condition your body to the changing pattern," says Baron. "Add 15-minute increments because you need only make small adjustments to your waking hour schedule."

Meet a Customer Service Dazzler

GERRY GARTHE: 'PASS THAT HAPPINESS ALONG'

Is happiness contagious? Gerry Garthe thinks so. She says reps can find that out for themselves by spreading some of their good mood on to customers.

"Always try to convey happiness on the phone," suggests Garthe, a phone rep for Steelcase, Inc., in Grand Rapids, Michigan. "The more you try, the easier it will get. Your happy and positive attitude will spread to your customers quickly — even when you are cold calling. As a bonus, when the day is over, you will still feel fresh, and may even be upbeat for the commute home."

BANK'S BOTTOM LINE — FUN

Who is that guy in the cancan dress? At Phelps County Bank in Missouri, it might be one of the employees.

Phelps CEO Emma Lou Brent says workers' high level of commitment at Phelps had caused stress, reports *Business Ethics*. When bank employees stopped having fun, productivity declined. But now, the bank allows time for fun. Recently, male employees danced the cancan, in appropriate costumes, at a staff meeting.

Brent credits the initiatives with helping the bank reduce overhead 3 percent and increase net income by 32 percent. But no one is pressured to take part in any activity.

QUICK TIPS

- **Cut the fun on voice mail.** Fun and creativity are out and straight talk is in for voice mail and answering machines. Judith Martin, also known as "Miss Manners," says, "People are tired of amateur theater on the telephone." Drop the jokes, sappy ballads, and clever narratives, she advises. Just state your telephone number and ask people to leave a message.

- **Germ-free calling.** Use alcohol wipes to clean the mouthpiece of your phone. Cold germs collect there.

- **Reenact the toughest situations.** Follow the example of one company that stages a game of charades each month in which reps recreate their most difficult customer situations. Everyone has a good time, but there's an added benefit: Players demonstrate what went wrong and then exchange ideas of what to do next time.

- **Cash in on laughter.** Bank of America sponsors popular joke-telling contests among employees. One contestant said, "After the contest we come back to work so de-stressed, it must show in our work because I see a lot of happier customers that day."

- **Tackle that tough job.** Is there a tough, boring, or otherwise unpleasant project you've been putting off? Act immediately on it. You'll feel an instant reduction in stress by just getting over your procrastination.

- **Laugh: for the health of it.** A hearty laugh sends the adrenaline rushing. Hearts pump faster. Brains emit natural painkillers. Muscles relax. A good joke revs up the human motor and boosts productivity. So, go ahead. Enjoy a good laugh several times a day. Doctor's orders!

QUIZ

MANAGE YOUR ENERGY

Ann McGee-Cooper, a Dallas consultant, studied 3,500 people to assess their energy management levels. The following test is based on her findings. Circle one answer to each question.

1. Your midmorning break is most often spent:
   a. Complaining to a teammate about work problems.
   b. Taking care of such personal chores as letter writing.
   c. Relaxing and engaging in 'fun' activities.
   d. What morning break?

2. Times for fun and laughter:
   a. Occur primarily on weekends.
   b. Are deferred until your team reaches its goal.
   c. Happen many times a day at work and at home.
   d. Are mostly just a memory because of work.

3. On your commute home, your thoughts focus on:
   a. How pleasant the evening's social activities will be.
   b. All the work that you left unfinished.
   c. Your job problems and those waiting at home.
   d. The satisfaction you derived from the day's work.

4. When you get home, you usually:
   a. Take a walk or do some aerobic exercises.
   b. Lie on the couch all evening watching television.
   c. Force yourself to work more to reduce tomorrow's load.
   d. Make yourself a stiff drink.

HOW DOES YOUR ENERGY RATE?

Give yourself 10 points for each of the following circled answers: question 1, c; question 2, c; question 3, a or d; question 4, a. *Warning*: With a score of fewer than 20 points, you may be dangerously close to the burnout stage. Remember that while work is an important part of your life, it's still only a part. Relax!

YOUR DAZZLE ME! TAKE AWAY

HAVE FUN!

You're busy. The phones won't stop ringing, you've had to skip lunch, your stomach is in a knot, and the customer in front of you wants an answer *now*.

Welcome to the U.S. workplace of the '90s, where Americans consistently rank their jobs as the No. 1 source of stress in their lives, and where customer service ranks as the *8th* most stressful job in the nation. *Dazzle Me!* customer service reps know they do their best work when they're at their best. Take that as your cue to slow down, take a deep breath, and enjoy a good laugh with some friends.

WHAT YOU CAN DO *TODAY*

- **Look for the humor.** In at least one situation in which normally you are too stressed out to think "funny," try to find the humor in the situation. Share "war stories" with co-workers during your lunch break. Joel Goodman, director of The Humor Project, says, "People often say, 'Someday we'll laugh at this.' I say, 'Why wait?'"

- **Don't forget: Bosses like a smile, too.** In a survey for Accountemps, supervisors and managers were asked, *Do people with a sense of humor do better, the same as, or worse at their jobs than those with little or no sense of humor?* More than 95 percent said "better." (None said worse!) You'll feel better sharing a smile or humorous comment with your boss and you'll help lighten her stress for the day, too.

- **Laughter builds teamwork.** Bob Ross tells managers attending his seminars and reading his book *That's a Good One! Corporate Leadership with Humor* (Avant Books) to "ask yourself, what do a close-knit family, a championship team, and a thriving business organization have in common? First and foremost, the members enjoy being together, laughing, playing, and having fun making things happen."

- **Start a humor first-aid kit.** Stock it with things that make you laugh: cartoons, greeting cards, comedy tapes. Add any complimentary letters you've received from customers or co-workers. Pull it out "as needed" for stress relief.

- **Just laugh!** Keep in mind the words of psychologist William James: "We don't laugh because we're happy — we're happy because we laugh."

INDEX

N

O

P

Q